Leading
the Way

Carol A. Balfe
Science Literacy for All Children
5025 Werner Ct.
Oakland, CA 94602

▶ ▶ ▶

Leading the Way

**Principals and Superintendents
Look at Math Instruction**

Edited by Marilyn Burns

MATH SOLUTIONS PUBLICATIONS

Sausalito, California

Math Solutions Publications

A division of

Marilyn Burns Education Associates

150 Gate 5 Road, Suite 101

Sausalito, CA 94965

http://www.mathsolutions.com

Appendix A and appendix B to chapter 1 are reprinted with special permission from the Institute for Learning, Learning Research and Development Center, University of Pittsburgh.

Library of Congress Cataloging-in-Publication Data

Leading the way : principals and superintendents look at math
  instruction / edited by Marilyn Burns.
    p. cm.
  ISBN 0-941355-21-7 (pbk.)
   1. Mathematics—Study and teaching. 2. School administrators.
I. Burns, Marilyn 1941–   .
QA11.L385 1999
510'.71—dc21   99-31755
                                               CIP

Editor: Toby Gordon
Copy editor: Alan Huisman

Production: Alan Huisman
Cover and interior: Ron Kosciak, Dragonfly Design

Composition: Cape Cod Compositors, Inc.

Printed in the United States of America
  00 01 02 03 04 05 06 07 08   10 9 8 7 6 5 4 3 2

A Message from Marilyn Burns

We at Marilyn Burns Education Associates believe that teaching mathematics well calls for continually reflecting on and improving one's instructional practice. Our Math Solutions Publications include a wide range of choices, from books that describe problem-solving lessons, to *Math By All Means* units that show how to teach specific topics, to resources that help link math with writing and literature, to children's books that help students develop an appreciation for math while learning basic concepts.

Along with our large collection of teacher resource books, we have a more general collection of books, videotapes, and audiotapes that can help teachers and parents bridge the gap between home and school. All of our materials are available at education stores, from distributors, and through major teacher catalogs.

In addition, Math Solutions Inservice offers five-day courses and one-day workshops throughout the country. We also work in partnership with school districts to help implement and sustain long-term improvement in mathematics instruction in all classrooms.

To find a complete listing of our publications and workshops, please visit our Web site at www.mathsolutions.com. Or contact us by calling (800) 868-9092 or sending an e-mail to info@mathsolutions.com. We'd be pleased to send you a copy of our complimentary Math Solutions Newsletter in which we share teaching ideas, new resources, student work, and information about important issues concerning math education.

We're eager for your feedback and interested in learning about your particular needs. We look forward to hearing from you.

A DIVISION OF MARILYN BURNS EDUCATION ASSOCIATES

Contents

Leaders on the Road to Change

Marilyn Burns

Teachers are the key to children's math learning, the conduits between the child and the math curriculum. In schools across the country, principals face an important challenge—how to help teachers in all classrooms become more effective in their teaching of mathematics. Professional books and staff development seminars can help teachers think in new ways and offer them improved instructional strategies and approaches. But while professional development may result in improved mathematics instruction in individual classrooms, long-lasting, schoolwide change calls for substantive, ongoing, schoolwide support. For this to happen, the leadership of the building principal is essential.

How best to support math instruction in schools is a complex issue. Principals' curriculum responsibilities extend far beyond mathematics. In most elementary schools, the literacy curriculum sits up front. Literacy is our nation's primary focus, as it should be. Fortunately, attention to improving the teaching of reading and writing can have a positive impact on the teaching of all subjects, mathematics included.

But unlike teaching language arts, teaching mathematics effectively often includes an extra hurdle—the content. Teachers (especially elementary teachers) have math backgrounds that are typically weak and often woeful, and the math expertise in elementary schools is generally minimal—few teachers are interested in mathematics and/or well prepared mathematically. This makes the principal's challenge all the more complex, especially if the principal is also someone for whom math is not a particular strength. In addition, principals' responsibilities are much wider than the curriculum; they manage all programs related to the school.

However, only when attention to and support for math instruction become a daily aspect of teachers' lives at school will we see any progress in helping children become comfortable, skilled mathematicians. And just as there's no one way for teachers to teach math effectively, there isn't just one way for principals to be instructional leaders in this area.

Most schools and districts regularly adopt new instructional materials, and math takes its turn along with the other curriculum areas. It's also common for principals to observe math lessons. Yet the impact of these two practices is usually insufficient to produce improved instruction. Faced with the pressure of district tests, the scarcity of math leadership, and limited funds, principals have had to search for other ways to support the math teaching in their schools.

This book offers six stories of how administrators worked to improve mathematics instruction in their school district. Five of the chapters are written by principals of elementary schools: one in New York City, one in San Francisco, one in Bellevue (Washington), and two in Tucson. The sixth chapter is jointly written by the superintendent and the director of elementary math and science education in Hudson, Massachusetts. I came to know many of these administrators through their participation in the courses and workshops offered by Math Solutions Inservice, and I'm pleased to have been able to support them in their efforts.

Each situation is unique, and so is the approach each of these administrators took to improving the teaching of mathematics. But common to all the stories is the knowledge that improving mathematics instruction is a complex task that requires ongoing attention. In that spirit, all of the chapters are works in progress, in which the authors describe how they arrived at where they are now while realizing that the work is never finished.

To begin, Anna Switzer, principal of P. S. 234, in New York City's District Two, describes how she has relied heavily on professional development to improve math instruction in her school, beginning in 1992. As a result of this support, teachers took ownership of their mathematics instruction and the school eventually became a "collaborative" site, with other district teachers coming to observe and study mathematics and math teaching. Along with the attention it has paid to classroom instruction, P. S. 234 has developed a schoolwide program for students at risk. Realizing that change is an ongoing process, Anna now feels she needs to turn serious attention to refining the school's math curriculum, increasing efforts to involve parents, and finding ways to continue supporting teachers and helping them avoid burnout.

Rita Lowy, of Ardmore Elementary School, a K–5 school in the Bellevue School District, near Seattle, Washington, comes to the job of principal after teaching high school mathematics for more than twenty years. Therefore, she has a special expertise in mathematics to offer her faculty. Rita works closely with classroom teachers to improve their mathematics instruction, and she describes the specifics of observing lessons, holding pre- and postobservation conferences with teachers, and helping teachers think about preparing lessons.

Bob Wortman is principal of Borton Primary Magnet School, a small inner-city K–2 school operating under court-ordered desegregation in the Tucson (Arizona) Unified School District. The school has been recognized for its exemplary literacy programs, and Bob relates how he has turned the school's attention to mathematics, basing the effort on the same principles that guided their progress in literacy. Bob describes how constructivist learning parallels teaching changes. He outlines

Brian Cambourne's "conditions for learning"—immersion, demonstration, engagement, expectation, responsibility, use, approximation, and response—and explains how all are essential for a school dedicated to systemic change.

In 1988, when Judith Rosen became principal of Jefferson School, a K–5 school in the San Francisco Unified School District, in California, she found a school that was very traditional in its approach to teaching math. Her goal was to get her faculty to embrace and implement the guidelines of the Mathematics Framework for California Public Schools. Judith points to three reasons change took place at Jefferson—her ability to send clear messages to the faculty defining her math goals for the school, her recognition that professional development is crucial, and her effort toward developing a collaborative and collegial staff. Recognizing that systemic change takes years, Judith shares some of the details in her own change from school manager to curriculum leader as she talks about the journey she and the school are taking together.

Rosanna Gallagher describes her experience as principal of Drachman Primary Magnet School, a school for K–3 children in the Tucson (Arizona) Unified School District. Believing that the principal must set the tone for the school, Rosanna explains how she works toward being a flexible visionary. She defines the principles that guide her efforts toward improving mathematics instruction, which include arranging for professional growth opportunities for all teachers, modeling being a learner and risk taker, building a team approach among the faculty, honoring the key role of classroom teacher, and believing that anything is possible.

Sheldon Berman is the superintendent of Hudson Public Schools, in Hudson, Massachusetts, and Arthur Camins is the director of elementary mathematics and science. In their chapter, they spell out their vision of what math education should look like and what's needed for systemwide, systemic reform. They describe the district's shift from one in which the teachers designed their own (inconsistent) math curriculum to one with a well-defined instructional math program. They reveal the tensions that developed as a result of the change, the various entry points they provided to support teachers at different levels of experience, the kinds of administrative support they offered, and the involvement of school committees. Their chapter includes details about how they plan to sustain and refine the program's implementation over the next few years, maintaining the program's integrity while enabling teachers to modify and adjust it.

Seeing how others approach a task is always beneficial. I know you will find practical ideas in these stories that will help your school on its own journey to an effective math curriculum, one accessible to all students and one that produces citizens who can comfortably and proficiently take on the mathematical aspects of daily life.

1

Math Conversions:
One Principal's Story

Anna Switzer

Anna Switzer is the principal of P. S. 234, a K–5 school in the heart of TriBeCa (an abbreviation of "*Tri*angle *Be*low *Ca*nal" Street), a fast-growing New York City community. TriBeCa's primarily white population comprises artists (the area is famous for its converted lofts), professionals (many of whom live in Battery Park City), municipal workers, and skilled laborers. New York City encourages schools, when possible, to accept children whose parents work in the neighborhood, and P. S. 234 is thus able to enroll more African American and Hispanic children then it might otherwise; there has also been a recent surge in the number of Asian children. The school has 650 students in twenty-three classes. Average class size is twenty-eight in kindergarten through grade 3 and thirty-two in grades 4 and 5.

became the principal of P. S. 234 in 1992. I had come to the school four years earlier as a staff developer, after having been a kindergarten teacher. I spent those four years learning the administrative and supervisory ropes and working on improving instruction. In our brand of progressive education, we set up multiage classes in which the children remained with the same teacher for two years, we didn't use textbooks (except in math), and teachers and students called one another by their first name. More important, we emphasized process over product, resisted attempts toward skill and drill, and did not sort the students according to ability or any other classification. Wishing to maintain the integrity and distinctive qualities of the school, I was not planning any major changes now that I was principal.

The former principal (and my mentor and friend), Blossom Gelernter, was very knowledgeable about mathematics education, but math was an area in which I, like many principals and teachers, was unsure of myself. Blossom had always subscribed to the idea that children should understand what they are doing. Our students worked with Cuisenaire rods, base ten blocks, pattern blocks, and tangrams. Teachers had read and used Mary Baratta-Lorton's *Mathematics Their Way* (Addison-Wesley, 1976), as well as the Nuffield math books (*Nuffield Mathematics Project*, Newgate Press Limited, 1971). We felt a certain confidence in our approach.

The July before I was going to be in charge officially I decided to join four other teachers in attending a Math Solutions 1 course presented by Marilyn Burns Education Associates (MBEA). I thought this would be a good way as a new principal to learn more about mathematics, but I wasn't for a moment expecting any radical insights.

I was full of the beginner's nervous energy and consumed with the challenges I knew lay ahead. I had always been either a teacher or a staff developer working very closely with teachers, so I felt totally at home with my staff. Every day for a week the four teachers and I commuted from my house in the country to the little town in Connecticut where the course was being held. It was a very happy week. We were away from all responsibilities of classes and families, free to talk shop all day. We began slowly (the first day we assumed we knew it all), but by the time Marilyn Burns spoke on Wednesday we were totally hooked. We wanted more, and I decided my first challenge as principal was to find ways to get more of this kind of math to P. S. 234.

Finding the resources and getting my superintendent and most of my district colleagues committed to a more authentic and powerful mathematics program was a slow and steady process. The district had devoted enormous energy to literacy, with impressive results, and was therefore primed to think about giving math more emphasis as well. Over the next five years a wonderful staff developer named Lucy West worked intensively with our teachers to refine and develop their math education. (After four years Lucy was appointed assistant principal and helped redefine that role, changing it from one of administrator to one of mentor teacher and professional developer.) Eventually I was able to hire another part-time staff developer, Ellen Foote, and with lots of help from our own staff and MBEA, we transformed our school and our district. Marilyn Burns, always a critical friend, coached us and cheered us on.

Creating an Atmosphere for Change

One of the most difficult things a principal has to do is decide which initiatives are worthwhile and which are not, which ones will be easy for her school to adapt and which will divide the staff. In an era where so much information is dispersed daily, where there are so many programs clamoring for your attention—and your dollar—the best choices are those that are within your reach and that reflect your and your staff's true beliefs about how children learn.

The success or failure of an innovative education program is determined more by whether it upholds or challenges the school community's beliefs than by the number or breadth of the changes involved. If the teachers believe that children learn by being told, then it is easier to introduce a new curriculum built upon telling than it is to introduce ideas that depend on children's making their own discoveries. If, on the other hand, the teachers believe that children (and adults) learn best by building meaning for themselves, then it is far easier to introduce a math initiative that dispenses with memorized formulas. In this respect we are fortunate. Most of our staff members believe that children learn best by doing and that the differences children bring to learning are a source of strength.

Time is also a critical factor in change. In New York, the curriculum can be changed overnight by the school chancellor's decree, but implementing it is slow going in schools where 90 percent of the day's activities are predetermined and there is no time for meetings and discussions. One is mistaken in thinking one can change a school's practice in any meaningful way in a short time. Being creative about time for talking and planning is a constant challenge.

A third factor is trust. Trust between teachers and teacher leaders needs to develop in order for educators to consider changing their practice significantly. Trust means that both teachers and leaders have discovered that it is safe to take risks and chances, safe to make mistakes in front of one another in a protected environment. Often our mistakes are what propel us. A lesson gone wrong is an opportunity rich with possibilities for dissection and discussion.

Making It Happen

All principals are familiar with the basic elements of staff development, as captured in the acronym COWBIRD. As Lucy
guided us through day-to-day conferences, observations,
workshops, bulletins, intervisitations, reading, and demonstrations, I learned important lessons about leadership and the
ways and means of supporting growth and change. Becoming
an effective principal meant feeling and behaving as if almost
anything was within my reach if I cared enough about it. It
wasn't that it was easy—it was part of the work. Sometimes it
meant cajoling the deputy superintendent into a larger budget
for staff development; sometimes it meant finding the time to
write a proposal for a math retreat; sometimes it meant per-
suading parents that it was worth their time to come to math
night. I passed this lesson down to the staff: they too needed a
can-do attitude toward whatever would make change possible.

I began to see my job as principal as yes-woman. If
someone made a reasoned request, I said yes. Over the next
five years I requisitioned thousands of interlocking cubes,
hired hundreds of substitutes so that teachers could visit one
another's classrooms and classrooms in other schools, purchased scores of books on mathematics and mathematics education. Calculators were everywhere, and each class got an
overhead projector to use during whole-class discussions. I

met often and eagerly with teachers who were unsure, unready, recalcitrant, or reluctant to keep moving forward. I shifted teachers to different grades. I changed schedules to accommodate meetings, workshops, and joint planning. I read articles and books, spoke to colleagues, and corresponded regularly with Marilyn Burns. I studied our math tests—before they were given, to know better how to prepare the children, and after they had been taken, to understand better where we needed more work. I met with parents individually and in groups to defend a teacher's practice and the school's philosophy. We had visitors, visitors, and more visitors. And through it all I often found myself confused and conflicted. Should we really abandon all algorithms? Should we move more slowly? Did we need more balance between the old and the new? I undertook yet more conversations and more correspondence. I worked hard, and everyone else did too.

Lucy and I attempted to give teachers whatever support they needed. Some chose to meet with Lucy every week; others planned new units together and shared the responsibility of teaching them. Lucy and I together decided which teachers to encourage to be very bold, which ones to advise to think smaller and slow down. Some staff members took courses with Lucy when she taught at Bank Street College, others went each summer to another Math Solutions course. (In fact, we became the district host school for MBEA for six summers.)

We designed at least one parent night a year dedicated to building understanding and approval of our mathematics program. There is no better way for teachers to learn what they believe than to prepare to explain their curriculum and its purpose to a group of parents. Over time we noted less resistance from parents to abandoning the math curriculum they were familiar and comfortable with and more understanding on their part for how math education had to change if their children were to be successful in the next century. The upshot was that when the district mandated using *Investigations*, a TERC-designed curriculum published by Dale Seymour, we were able to do so without much of a struggle.

After two or three years of this kind of training and experience, teachers at P. S. 234 no longer felt they were doing "Marilyn Burns math" or "TERC math" or "Math in the City" (a program sponsored by the City University of New York). While all these curricular aids were extremely helpful to us in thinking about and developing our mathematics program, they no longer defined us—we had taken ownership of the ideas and materials and created a curriculum that belonged to us, looked like us, and met our specific needs.

Inside most children is a strong mathematician waiting to be freed. Anyone spending time in our classrooms today sees kids actively working on mathematics with a much different focus than in the past. They are conducting whole-class investigations *(In the Middle Ages what percentage of the land was owned by what percentage of the population?)*, working cooperatively in small groups, solving authentic problems *(How much bigger is the harp seal than the ringed seal? How many bulbs will we need to ring the perimeter of our school garden with tulips?)*, doing math mentally, learning estimation techniques, using calculators when appropriate, thinking flexibly about number *(How will we celebrate the one-hundredth day of school mathematically?)*, and dealing with probability, measurement, geometry, and pattern. Math blocks of at least one hour are now scheduled four or five times a week, almost always first thing in the morning. Children are expected to write about their work in clear and organized detail. Lots of strategies are used to get to any answer, if indeed there is one right answer to a problem. The work is rich, deep, and often joyful. Many of our children declare that math is their favorite subject.

Expanding the Arena

Our efforts have been influential in causing the district to adopt a more constructivist mathematics model. Three years ago the superintendent suggested that P. S. 234 become a demonstration-collaboration site where other district teachers could come to observe and study mathematics and mathematics education. This was heady confirmation that the district had confidence in us and wanted us to take a leader-ship role in changing the district's mathematics program. Lucy and I were excited and eager to begin. But our teachers told us they weren't yet ready. They felt their reputation was on the line. It was one thing to try new things with children or ask their peers to coach them. It was entirely different to invite unknown district colleagues to observe and criticize them. So, to everyone's credit, we put it off until we had worked longer at changing and refining our practice.

Over the next year and a half, however, the superinten-dent's proposal was realized. Now each year, on seven or eight separate days, as many as fifty teachers from other schools in the district come to our school to meet our teachers, observe them teach, and discuss what they see. Each day is tightly struc-tured and very carefully planned. During the first forty-five min-utes, everyone meets as a group and discusses the lessons being taught that day. The visiting teachers then spend an hour in each of two classrooms watching the lessons unfold. (Lucy and Ellen have prepared guidelines to help teachers focus these observa-tions; see appendix A.) After that all the teachers and staff devel-opers have lunch together and spend most of the afternoon discussing the lessons and making comments or suggestions (again, there are guidelines to help focus these discussions; see appendix B). If there is time, everyone works on a math problem together or discusses plans for future sessions.

Our decision to call the school a *collaboration site* rather than a *demonstration site* was a good—and very conscious—one. We do not want to set ourselves up as "experts" but simply to ask other district teachers to join us as we all develop more expertise. (See the "welcome" letter in appendix C.) As a result there is little resentment from either the hosting or visiting teachers and very little negative criticism. Our plan is that over the next few years a number of other schools will become collaboration sites as well.

Last December we hosted a daylong conference on mathematics for all the principals in the district. The conference was fashioned after our collaboration-site meetings—the principals spent the day learning about math instruction by observing our teachers teach and talking with them before and after the lessons. They also had an opportunity to ask questions about what changes had been made and where we still wanted to go. The principals now understand what their teachers do on these "math visits" and why it is worthwhile to hire substitutes and encourage their teachers to take advantage of professional development opportunities.

Zeroing In on Students at Risk

As we have been able to look at math more closely, we have begun to zero in on the way children learn math and have gotten better at helping children for whom understanding math is a challenge. Sometimes we are able to provide more attention to those children during the math lesson; sometimes we provide special sessions for those children.

Last year Lucy West worked with seven district teachers (five of whom were from our school) to create a remedial math program. After months of planning and design, our first group of fifteen third graders began a seven-week after-school math program consisting of twice-a-week one-and-a-half-hour sessions. For the pilot program we trained a number of high school students (their school is across the street) in how to present the activities so that the younger children would make their own discoveries and come to their own conclusions. The high school students then worked with the third graders one-on-one or in small groups. In addition we hired a teacher to observe every session.

By next fall we hope to have similar after-school classes in place for second and fourth graders. We're also discussing summer sessions. And we're working on instituting these special sessions in all the schools in the district.

Where We Are Now

Lucy West has moved on to become the district math coordinator. Because of the knowledge and experience she has gained through her many years of working with children and teachers, she has great influence over the district's teachers and principals and continues to be a vital instrument for change. Our latest challenge is to allow and encourage great teachers to remain in the classroom and at the same time bring about more staff development in the district's schools.

Our need for math staff developers grows faster than our ability to train them. Once again we've had to come up with some unique solutions. Our plan next year is to free three or four P. S. 234 teachers from their classroom one day a week so that they can work in other schools as math staff developers. They will be paid for the extra time they spend planning for and following up on their staff-development assignments. If we hire one or two "adjunct" teachers as regular substitutes, we'll be able to maintain continuity in these classrooms. Each adjunct will spend two days a week in the classroom, the day before as well as the day of their substitute assignment. (The costs associated with this plan will be absorbed by the district in lieu of hiring a district math staff developer.)

Our novel solutions to the challenges of better instruction are energizing. The school is being responsive to the needs of its community by creating opportunities. Teachers, rather than burning out, see themselves as leaders with unlimited possibilities. Children now have many more opportunities to learn.

The more holistic approach to mathematics we are taking fits in with the beliefs we already hold about how children learn—constructively—how staff members need to work together—collaboratively—and how groups and classes should be organized—cooperatively. By designing more open-ended, discovery-based lessons, emphasizing other mathematical strands besides number (geometry, data, measurement, probability, and pattern), and becoming more knowledgeable about mathematics and mathematical pedagogy, we see our essential beliefs played out every day.

Here's how it works: give children real problems; allow them to interact with others while working on these problems; give them opportunities to use different materials and strategies to solve the problems; expect them—and give them the time—to share their discoveries; respect the many ways they come to understand the world; and allow them to demonstrate that understanding in a variety of ways—pictures, numbers, words.

The children have fallen in love with what they are finding in mathematics, and teachers, parents, and I have too. The inventiveness of the work our students produce gives us new insights into how they think and often delights us. Although a few teachers have reservations about some of the changes, the resistance has more to do with how to do it all rather than why do it. This is authentic learning in student-centered classrooms, and we are all very certain of its benefits, not the least of them being that our students' scores on standardized math tests continue to rise.

Mistakes, Concerns, and Unresolved Questions

Of course, we made mistakes along the way. And we're entitled to: if we weren't, we'd never undertake anything new. The best part of making mistakes is that your friends and colleagues don't have to make the same ones if you are generous about sharing your recently earned expertise. Here are some of our mistakes and what we learned from them:

1. Don't think you can do extensive math work without a chalkboard: uncover those boards! You need lots of writing space to do math.

2. Repeatedly asking kids to "find more ways" to solve a problem isn't always the best direction. After a few strategies the remaining solutions may be obtuse and ineffective. And a solution that is clever or inventive for an eight-year-old is inefficient or unwieldy for a ten-year-old. Teachers need to know when to guide and when to follow.

3. "Show your work" doesn't mean a child should write pages and pages of number or word explanations for

simple calculations they did in their head simply because they're afraid they'll lose credit if they leave anything out. Children need to see examples of organized papers, mostly those of other children. There also needs to be time for you to ask them what they are trying to communicate, time for respectful comments and questions from their peers.

4. You can tell children to practice a specific strategy once in a while. "Today let's find the best answers by grouping by tens." "Jenny did this by doubling. I'd like everyone to try it that way." This is not authoritarian or anticonstructivist. It's an advantage to have a teacher in the room: she or he often knows something a child might not.

5. Share your specific goals with parents. When your local newspaper writes that your math program doesn't expect third graders to memorize the multiplication tables, for example, don't panic; make your expectations clear and public.

Another concern shared by many educators is that their students—those who excel as well as those who fall behind—are being tutored without their knowledge or approval. These tutors often use methods that differ from or conflict with the ones being used at school, which can cause a lot of confusion.

Last year on the fifth-grade performance test in mathematics we were disappointed in some of the computational strategies students chose to use, which included algorithms they had not learned at school. We also found that the students frequently used those algorithms incorrectly and without the good sense they usually employed when estimating or doing mental math. Should we be upset that parents and tutors are teaching children these formulas incorrectly? Should we teach the procedures ourselves in the hope that the students will put those procedures to better use? Should we just ignore it?

We do not have all the answers. But we know the kinds of discussions we need to have about them. Feeling proud of the work we have done is empowering. Bringing others into the conversation and the work means there are more people to help us find answers. We are still adding it up.

Appendix A
Preobservation Focus Questions

1. **What are the goals of the lesson?** What mathematical concepts, problem-solving techniques, reasoning, skills, tools, is the teacher trying to highlight? How and why has the teacher made adaptations to the TERC lesson?

2. **What is the content of the lesson in relation to its goals and the students' prior knowledge?** What prior knowledge does the lesson build on? In what ways does the teacher expect students to present and discuss their ideas and products? How does the teacher expect to know whether students understand and have successfully learned? What constitutes evidence of students' understanding and reasoning?

3. **What assistance does the teacher anticipate the students will need during the lesson?** What kinds of mechanisms and expectations for collaboration are in place? What kind of individual assistance is anticipated? What mechanisms and structures are in place that support students' autonomy and independence?

Appendix B
Postobservation Questions

1. **Were the goals of the lesson achieved?** In what ways were students encouraged and required to communicate their understanding and thinking? What was the evidence that students *did reach* the goals of the lesson? Is there evidence that students *did not meet* the objectives?

2. **How did the teacher support students in reaching the lesson's objectives?** Did the lesson encourage collaboration? Did the classroom discussion take place in an atmosphere of mutual respect? How were students' contributions valued? Were students supported and pushed to discuss matters relevant to the goals of the lesson? What questions fostered students' thinking? How were difficulties, confusions, and misconceptions revealed by the students addressed?

3. **What is planned for future lessons?**

Appendix C
Mathematics Initiative
Welcome Letter

Welcome to the Mathematics Initiative Collaboration Site at P. S. 234! The classes at P. S. 234 are heterogeneously grouped and, except for grades 4 and 5, multiaged. We expect children to function at different levels and to accept each person's unique contribution to the community.

Our practice is based on certain values:

- Autonomy and independence of students coupled with a willingness to help or ask for help when needed.

- Diversity of approaches and an effort to understand one another's thinking through active listening.

- Curiosity and a healthy skepticism as evidenced by a willingness to ask questions, to disagree, to consider other opinions, and to look for proof.

- Patience and mutual respect.

- A spirit of collaboration and cooperative behavior coupled with personal responsibility.

- Hard work and perseverance.

- The delight of learning.

Because we are always working to refine our practice, we would like feedback about how our practice supports the values we espouse and where it may contradict our stated values. We would like to engage in a dialogue with you that will allow all of us to grow and refine the teaching and learning that takes place at our schools.

Remember that your presence in the classroom can have a considerable impact on the direction of the lesson and on the manner in which children interact with one another and the teacher. We would like everyone in the room to be involved in an experience that is as close as possible to an authentic lesson. That means that the teacher (or coteachers) are the only adults responsible for managing the lesson and acting on observations and that the children are interacting with one another and their teacher(s). Therefore, please:

- Distribute yourselves around the room so that children can maneuver around you easily and so that you will have a variety of perspectives to share when you get together later to share observations.

- Resist interacting with children. If children ask you questions about the math, suggest that they talk with their partners first or find other classmates who can help.

- Spend sufficient time (at least five minutes) with a single small group in order to get a good sense of the children's thinking before you move to another group. Record your observations to share later.

- Resist having conversations among yourselves in the classroom. Instead, record your questions, reflections, etc., to share later.

Sincerely,

Lucy West
Ellen Foote

2

The Principal as Coach

Rita Lowy

Rita Lowy is the principal of Ardmore Elementary School, kindergarten through grade 5. Ardmore is part of the Bellevue School District, near Seattle, Washington. Enrollment is currently 420 students, about fifty of whom come from outside the neighborhood. A third of the student body speak English as a second language (the first language of these students is primarily Japanese, Chinese, or Korean, although there is also a rapidly growing Hispanic and Eastern European population). A third of the student body are also entitled to the benefits of Title I programs, and 40 percent receive a free or reduced-price lunch.

After teaching high school mathematics for over twenty years—work I loved—I obtained my administrative credentials and became an assistant principal in a large urban high school. Two years spent dealing primarily with schedules, discipline, and attendance convinced me this wasn't the career for me. My teaching life had been rooted in classroom instruction, and that's where my heart still lingered. But I longed to be able to impact the learning of a larger number of students than a single classroom.

Intrigued and impressed with the hard work my daughter was doing as an elementary school teacher, I began to wonder whether I could be an effective instructional leader at that level. Eager for the challenge, I applied for a position as the principal of a K–5 elementary school in my urban district. I got the job, and am beginning my fifth year.

Starting Out

When I arrived at the school, I learned that the teachers designed their own mathematics curriculum. District learning objectives and frameworks were in place, and teachers received clear guidelines and parameters about planning problem-based lessons. Classrooms were stocked with materials, cupboards were packed with resource books and replacement units. So far so good.

But I wasn't at my new school very long before I realized there was a problem: many trained teachers were retiring, their replacements didn't have the experience or training to design a math program, and too many others didn't understand that the activities by themselves did not add up to a comprehensive program.

I also discovered that "problem-based instruction" meant different things to different teachers. While some teachers were adept at using problems to help students learn important concepts, others were focusing on the problems, not on the concepts their students were to learn. In some classrooms, problems and activities had no clear instructional goals other than to engage the students.

The Road to Good Teaching

Decisions made while planning, executing, and reflecting on a lesson are at the heart of good teaching. In "The Basic Teaching Skill: Decision Making" (Research and Development Memorandum No. 104, Center for Research and Development in Teaching, Stanford University School of Education, 1973), Richard Shavelson says, "Any teaching act is a result of a decision, whether conscious or unconscious, that the teacher makes after the complex cognitive processing of available information. This reasoning leads us to the hypothesis that *the basic teaching skill is decision making*" (p. 18).

Since good questioning is a way to coach teachers on how to make good decisions, I felt I needed to come up with questions that would get the teachers in my school thinking in the right direction. The best setting for raising these questions seemed to be in connection with my classroom observations, which now include both a preobservation conference and a postobservation conference.

Preobservation Questions

Teachers come to a preobservation conference having prepared answers to these questions:

1. What preceded the lesson to be observed that prepares the students for the new learning you will be presenting?

2. What concept do you want the students to learn in this lesson?

3. What specific activity will you use to introduce children to the concept?

4. How can you best give directions for the activity so that all students understand what they must do? (Will model-

ing the activity for the class let you know whether everyone understands the activity?)

5. How much time will you spend talking about the activity afterward so that you can assess student learning and summarize the concept they are exploring? (What is the balance between activity and group discussion?)

6. What evidence will the students be able to provide that will tell you what they've learned?

7. What questions will you ask to nudge students' thinking about the concept's purpose and significance?

8. What problems do you anticipate and how will you overcome them?

9. What homework will you give to motivate the next day's lesson, extend the current lesson, or emphasize the concept you want the students to learn?

Although these questions are generic, they encourage a teacher to focus on the concepts she wants her students to learn and the questions she can use to prod their thinking. Answering these questions lets her structure the lesson, think ahead of time of the kinds of questions she'll want to ask, decide what evidence will tell her that student learning has occurred, and plan what she will do to follow up.

Postobservation Questions

The postconference questions are designed to promote reflection:

1. How would you summarize your impressions of the lesson? Did you accomplish what you set out to do?

2. What are your impressions based on? What did the students do that led you to conclude that they grasped the concept?

3. Did the lesson take a direction you did not expect?

4. How did your decisions and your behavior affect the lesson? (What is your hunch about what caused _____ _____?
   Why do you think the students _____?
   What was your role in making _____
   happen?)

5. What did you learn about your students? What insights can you apply to future experiences?

Working It Out

Perhaps an example of how I interacted with one teacher, Emily, last year will make all this more concrete. In the first of her lessons I observed, Emily posed the following problem to her fourth and fifth graders: how long would it take for an ant to crawl out of a twelve-foot well if it climbed four feet during the day and dropped two feet at night? She asked the children to solve the problem, draw a picture, and explain the solution in words, all worthy requirements. Pictures and diagrams are tools for solving problems, and writing can help students gain a deeper understanding of their thinking.

Emily responded to the children who raised their hands with questions, but the others received little direction or support. As the children worked, I noticed Thai drawing a picture of an ant thinking about the problem. Carlos drew a picture of a well with the ant bowing atop it (waiting for applause, I presumed). For many of the children, the pictures were an add-on, not an aid for solving the problem.

When everyone had finished, the students lined up in front of Emily, one by one, and she checked their work. M.J. showed Emily his explanation, diagram, and incorrect approach: *12 ÷ 2 = 6.* Since it was clear that his diagram could have led him to the correct solution, Emily asked him to go back and keep trying. With Emily's permission, I asked M.J. a question: could he show me how the diagram gave him the answer? He scratched his head all the way back to his desk. After studying the diagram for a few more minutes, he had the solution: the ant would be out of the hole by the end of the fifth day.

Afterward, I asked Emily about her goals for the lesson. Had she accomplished them? What important concepts did the children learn? How was this lesson connected to her learning objectives for the students? Her answers were vague. When I asked what her focus had been, she said she wanted the students to solve the problem and to be able to explain their solution through a drawing and in writing. I suggested that if she limited the focus of the lesson to using diagrams to solve problems, she could guide the students to think of their diagram as a way to delineate the elements of the problem and help them solve it, not simply as an illustration.

Then we talked about how thinking and reasoning need to be the overarching goal for every lesson, how developing good probing questions is a major part of a teacher's planning. I also suggested that she use the student work produced during the lesson to generate a class conversation that would nudge the students toward new awareness.

Not long afterward I observed another lesson in Emily's class, in which she used fraction strips to develop the concept of portions of a whole. I noticed the students seemed excited about their hands-on work with the fraction strips. Several of them noted with surprise that one third was larger than one fourth. They were beginning to construct some understanding of the relationship between various fractional parts. In the course of the lesson, the children played several fraction-strip games, but I couldn't tell whether they understood the relationship between the numerators and denominators of the fractions. The activity had again become the lesson. And once again, there was no class discussion in which the children could share observations they may have had about their work.

Over the year, however, responding to my persistent questioning, Emily made some positive changes. She began to focus on the learning goals she had for her students and on how to tell whether they had achieved them. This is often a difficult task for teachers, particularly those who themselves struggle with mathematics. Emily and I talked a lot about how to get students to understand mathematical concepts. We also talked about focusing clearly on what she wanted her students to be able to accomplish after a mathematics lesson or unit. I suggested that she ask herself these questions:

- What would I like the children to be able to do after a mathematics unit?

- What concepts must they understand in order to be able to do it?

- What activities or lessons will help them develop these concepts?

- What resources do I have to help me plan such lessons?

- What problems do I anticipate along the way?

- How can I best assess understanding day by day?

By the end of the year, Emily had markedly improved the way she planned and executed her lessons. Together, she and I planned a lesson on sorting and classifying quadrilaterals. How would she get the children to examine the properties of various four-sided shapes? How could she assess what the children already knew and at the same time trigger new learning? We talked through the questions I had been asking all along and decided on a partner activity in which students would sort paper quadrilateral shapes by various criteria—opposite sides congruent or not, consecutive sides congruent or not, opposite sides parallel, right angles, no right angles. After that Emily would define *quadrilateral, rhombus, square, trapezoid, rectangle,* and ask the students to write these labels on the appropriate paper shapes (some shapes would have only one label, others might have two or more). Two pairs of partners would then compare their work and report to the class. For homework, Emily would ask students to find pictures of each of the shapes in newspapers or magazines, classify them, and write a convincing argument for why they classified each picture as they did. The next day, Emily would introduce a geoboard activity involving quadrilateral shapes.

The lesson was a good model for Emily. She saw how it was deliberately prepared to achieve specific goals for student learning. She was delighted with the insights of the students and their work with the materials. She was most impressed with their thinking and their ability to express themselves when they advocated for their classifications.

After we had successfully planned another lesson together, Emily was able to continue on her own. Observing her in the classroom, I saw that she better understood the role of activities, problems, processing, and assessment in a lesson. She was honing her questioning skills and probing deeper into student thinking. (At the end of the year, she said she felt she could see into their brains!) Emily was on her way to being a highly effective mathematics teacher. Both she and I were proud of her accomplishments.

However, Emily's difficulties went beyond classroom planning. She had finally realized how uncomfortable she herself was with mathematics. That summer I sent Emily to a weeklong math educators' workshop, where she and other teachers learned mathematics and explored ways of delivering a comprehensive mathematics program. She came back confident and excited, saying she loved being a student, that activity-based mathematics was fun. And because some of the activities had been frustrating for her, she would now be better able to recognize those same feelings in her students. The class had increased her understanding of what math concepts need to be taught, introduced her to new ways to approach teaching those concepts, and given her ideas about how to assist the kids who really struggle.

Looking Back

This year I spoke with Emily about her experiences and feelings during the time we worked together. I needed feedback about how the support felt and how (or whether) it was helpful. I began by asking what was most frustrating to her about teaching math the year before.

"The biggest frustration was feeling like I was trying really hard to teach math, but not really knowing what good math instruction looked like," she replied. "I always questioned my effectiveness. I was teaching a new curriculum yet again. I felt like I was always only one step (or half a step) ahead of the kids."

She went on to say she felt I had been able to help her in several specific ways:

- "You pushed me to get more clarity on the goals and objectives of the math lessons I was teaching."

- "You gave me straightforward, honest feedback on the math teaching you saw me do."

- "You loaned me resources and reference books."

- "You suggested incorporating children's literature into my lessons as a way to begin or close a lesson and to illustrate an important point."

- "You gave me ideas for follow-up activities and homework."

- "You taught me about using questioning strategies to push students to do the problem solving themselves."

- "You supported my own learning by paying for me to attend a summer course and by having the positive presupposition that I would become a fine math teacher."

Emily summed up her experience working with me this way: "I found your support very helpful, because I was teaching a new grade level and was working with unfamiliar curriculum. Your support helped me become a more knowledgeable, intentional, and focused math teacher. I also found all the feedback somewhat scary and overwhelming, because it was the first time a principal had been that direct with me about the weaknesses of my teaching. I had feelings of inadequacy and failure, but then also a feeling that I would gain confidence and really be able to take pride in my teaching. Looking back on it, the most successful aspect was that I finally got some genuine feedback and direction to steer my math teaching in a stronger direction."

My work with Emily led me to some insights as well. First, teachers don't ask for help when they are struggling. In fact, many of them don't know they have a problem. Second, coaching takes time. I do between seventy and ninety observations a year, going into each classroom at least five times. When I see a teacher in trouble, I spend extra time with her. I observed Emily in her classroom fifteen times and spent many additional hours helping her plan lessons. Third, a trusting relationship with a teacher can only develop over time. I was the first principal who told Emily there might be a problem, who said everything wasn't just fine in her class. That isn't an easy thing for a teacher to hear, so it was important for me to set aside my "evaluator" hat and become a coach. By the same token, teachers must want to improve their work, and for her part, Emily understood that one immediate way she could improve her instructional skills was by accepting my support.

The principal is a most important partner in creating a classroom environment in which both students and teacher are thinking and learning. Giving teachers sound, honest feedback and asking them to reflect on what they do are the keys to changing weak instructional practices. Growth comes out of the trusting partnership of principals and teachers as well as of teacher peers. These relationships must be nurtured and encouraged. Anything less is an insult to your teachers' professionalism.

▶ ▶ ▶

3

Building Community Through Mathematics: The Principal's Role

Bob Wortman

Bob Wortman is the principal of Borton Primary Magnet School, a small inner-city K–2 school in an industrialized section of Tucson, Arizona. The school has complied with court-ordered desegregation for twenty years. The population of 240 students comprises 49 percent minority children (40 percent Hispanic, 8 percent African American, 1 percent Native American) from the surrounding economically depressed neighborhood and 51 percent bused-in middle-class European American children from across the 105 schools in the Tucson Unified School District. Almost 40 percent of the students are Spanish speakers, and 55 percent of the students receive a free or reduced-price lunch. Bob is also the author, with Myna Matlin, of *Leadership in Whole Language: The Principal's Role* (Stenhouse, 1995.)

It's the first day of school. I walk through the hallways and classrooms, welcoming new students and reassuring their nervous parents. I greet returning students and notice their new shoes and missing teeth, eavesdrop on their summer adventures. I am struck by the degree to which mathematics has become an integral part of our community-building practices:

- A kindergarten teacher is reading Diane Hamm's *How Many Feet in the Bed* (Simon and Schuster, 1991).

- In another kindergarten class, a small group of students is sorting and classifying all the unit blocks in the room so that they can be stored by shape and size.

- Another kindergarten teacher is letting her students explore a variety of math manipulatives.

- Second graders are graphing the number of letters in their names and recording data on the range, mean, median, and mode.

- Pairs of first and second graders are interviewing each other, drawing portraits, and constructing simple Venn diagrams to compare their similarities and differences.

- A multiage teacher has just read Sandra Cisneros's *Hair/Pelitos* (Knopf, 1984) to her first and second graders, and the students are gathering and recording data on hair length, color, and straight/wavy/kinky attributes.

- A first-grade class is discussing the calendar: *How many more days until your parents come for open house? How many days until the hundredth day of school?*

How, I think to myself, did mathematics come to be such a powerful context for building community during the first hour of the first day of the school year?

Background

Over its twenty-year existence, Borton has had only three principals, all holding postgraduate degrees in early childhood education and all having similar philosophical beliefs. I taught kindergarten and a kindergarten/first-grade multiage class at Borton for six years before returning as its principal. Over many years, the literacy practices in the school have changed to reflect current research and exemplary practices in the oral and written language development of first and second language students.

In contrast with the rich literature-based language arts program already in place when I became principal, the mathematics curriculum was presented through workbooks, worksheets organized around thematic studies, work stations, and pattern blocks and other manipulatives. Individually, all of these things are appropriate in the classroom, but a unifying belief system had not been articulated.

The teachers and I were unhappy with the vast difference between the engagement and quality of learning the children experienced during literacy versus math. The district's formal K–12 mathematics curriculum was loosely based on the NCTM strands, but the time allotted to various concepts in the school's ten classrooms varied greatly. Because we were unwilling to resort to the optional textbook provided by the district for all students in first grade and up, we began to make deliberate efforts to articulate and reflect on our beliefs about teaching and learning mathematics and to put our beliefs into action.

Constructivism and Teacher Change

In order to explain our struggles to align mathematics instruction more fully with NCTM standards, I need to explain my beliefs concerning school change as they apply to my role as an instructional leader. Constructivism is a theoretical model for understanding how children learn; it is also critical to understanding the change process in teaching. Constructivists believe that all people, adults and children alike, construct knowledge holistically, from the inside out, within the social context of the community of learners of which they are a part.

Teachers, as learners, construct new knowledge by building on their prior knowledge and experiences. Each staff member entering a building comes with a different background, different beliefs, and different experiences in mathematical understanding and mathematics instruction.

Piaget, in *The Language and Thought of the Child* (World, 1965), explains constructivism by proposing the dual concepts of *accommodation* and *assimilation* as continual processes always at work within the learner. As learners, we assimilate new ideas and concepts from our experiences and interactions while accommodating our ever changing internal structures to help us make continued sense of our world. Teachers continually choose either to assimilate new information and accommodate different activity structures into their existing practices or to discount them completely.

Equilibrium and *disequilibrium* are two additional constructivist notions that are critical to understanding the nature of educational change. Learners are in equilibrium when operating within their comfort zone. But when new experiences and ideas challenge existing views as to how our world is constructed, learners find themselves in a state of disequilibrium. Our most powerful learning takes place when we are at the edge, are in some degree of disequilibrium—when we must become more reflective and deliberate in our actions.

All teachers differ in terms of how close to the edge of

49

their learning they are willing to go before the fear of failure takes over. Teachers cannot be expected at once to "change" all aspects of their curriculum and the activities through which it is delivered.

Learners are also constantly incorporating new knowledge into an existing framework that is unique to them. Vygotsky, in *Thought and Language* (MIT, 1977), proposes that learning is socially constructed and that culture plays a powerful role in the construction of knowledge. He describes learning as socially contextualized and as the "connection" between prior knowledge and new knowledge. This concept of a "zone of proximal development" provides a special dimension to the learning process because it accounts for the role that a "teacher" plays.

Learning happens in an encounter between a novice and a more knowledgeable other. This relationship is not limited to that between a child and an adult. We all learn through our interactions with our peers. Teacher dialogue is the driving force behind professional development in the mathematics curriculum. Every teacher becomes an expert who can share his or her expertise with other staff members.

Constructivism Versus Behaviorism

Constructivism as a paradigm for explaining the learning process is in direct conflict with the more prevalent learning model of behaviorism. Behaviorism assumes that all learning can be broken into discrete, ultimately smaller bits of behavior that can be learned hierarchically. The individual pieces are learned from the outside in, as the isolated learner responds to positive and negative stimuli. Context plays a role only in the sense that the environment offers external rewards as feedback to the learner.

The notions of "readiness," "mastery," and "skills-based instruction" find their roots in behaviorism. The behaviorist paradigm describes part-to-whole learning and assumes that outside influences cause learning to happen. It is important for a behaviorist to provide positive reinforcement to the learner as she practices a skill over and over. The role of the behaviorist teacher (and principal) is to praise learning attempts and assess what skills need to be retaught. New knowledge has discrete, measurable, and prerequisite "pieces of learning" that have to be in place before it can be attempted. Mastery is real. It is something that can be succinctly identified as being reached. It is basically a deficit model of the learning process, always focusing on what is not learned.

The concept of "skills" from a constructivist view only has meaning as those skills relate to the larger context of learning. Constructivism is whole-to-part learning and always returns to the context of the whole. Learning within this paradigm isn't practicing a skill over and over, it's dealing with new concepts and ideas in a variety of contexts. Learning is a never ending process. The learner is never "getting ready" to learn but always in the process of learning. There will never be "mastery" in any real sense because there is always some new angle or fresh approach to a subject that can be considered. The role of teacher (and principal) is to help the learner identify areas of strength and areas in which he needs to grow and to provide resources and experiences that will help learning be meaningful.

Supporting Teacher Change

Having been a kindergarten/first-grade teacher for thirteen years before becoming a principal, I still find the classroom the most useful metaphor for thinking about school change. My beliefs about learning and my experience in the classroom help me frame my decisions when helping staff members in their professional growth. I equate the concept of "school change" with teacher learning. I believe that true change will occur only when we impact teacher learning. We can't force learning to happen from the outside in. We can only support learning in the individual from the inside out.

If I accepted the behaviorist paradigm, I would be pummeling my staff with workshop after workshop in mathematics, praising those who "caught on" and setting up remedial programs for those who didn't "get it." Everyone would be expected to teach mathematics in the same way and according to the standards set in the aforementioned workshops. Performance would be judged by outside experts, and I, as the administrator, would be held accountable for providing all the "pieces" for staff development.

But I ascribe to a constructivist model of learning. My staff is a social group of people with specific backgrounds and experiences who have a variety of strengths and areas in which they need to grow. I need to recognize them as individuals, help them reflect on their strengths and identify their areas for growth, and facilitate their learning. I am not the resident expert at everything. I cannot be the only teacher of teachers in my building. I must create an environment that supports a staff of teacher-learners who can respect one another's strengths and are willing to risk learning from one another. I must find the time, space, and money to facilitate ongoing communication. Workshops can introduce teachers to new ideas and strategies, but the cycle of reflection/dialogue/reflection/action is even more important. Teachers must see it happening in other classrooms and have the time to talk about how the instructional "piece" fits into the larger curriculum and the structure of the day.

Brian Cambourne, an Australian educator and researcher, has proposed a model for the way children learn language that applies to learning in general. His *The Whole Story: Natural Learning and the Acquisition of Literacy in the Classroom* (Scholastic, 1988) is an excellent basis for reflecting on the teacher as learner. I would like to frame my discussion of Borton's successful staff development practices around Cambourne's conditions for learning.

Immersion

In order for new knowledge and ideas to be internalized, the learner needs to be immersed in concepts and ideas at a variety of levels and in a variety of contexts. Learning mathematics is influenced by the nature and abundance of mathematical contexts the learner experiences. Teachers must be immersed in the strategies and ideas they are expected to use. Teachers and other staff members must be expected to share what they are reading, take part in professional discussions, and reflect continually on the ideas they encounter.

When I became Borton's principal, each of the teachers had taken a summer inservice seminar based on Mary Baratta-Lorton's book *Mathematics Their Way* (Addison-Wesley, 1976) and were implementing work stations in their classrooms to some degree. When Borton was selected to be an Exxon Staff Development School, several teachers attended Math Solutions 1, a weeklong summer program provided by

Marilyn Burns Education Associates. After several more summers, all the teachers had attended Math Solutions 1 and 2. Half of these teachers and I had also participated in Math Solutions 3.

We have also been able to meet and discuss issues with such outstanding constructivist theorists as Eleanor Duckworth, Constance Kamii, and Catherine Fosnot. These researchers have captured our imagination and pushed our thinking forward in ways that support us as we invent our own math program.

I find that the most fruitful, engaging inservice sessions are those that revolve around literature and math, perhaps because our teachers are so proficient and interested in literature that it seems a "safe" focus for everyone. It is the best route for us. While I can support individual inquiries in a variety of areas, literature provides a shared language and context for discussion.

Here are some other things we do at Borton:

- Each teacher is invited to join NCTM, and copies of *Teaching Children Mathematics* are available in the lounge.

- Teachers pass on articles that have influenced their thinking, and I see that copies are distributed to interested staff members.

- Our faculty meetings are held in a different classroom each week; the librarian tells us about new children's books and professional materials, and the host teacher shares successful ideas and strategies in mathematics.

- Every teacher chooses a professional book to read over the summer; in August they rate the resource as one that every teacher should have a copy of, that should be purchased for the school library, or that is not very useful.

- The district's Title I staff, through the Exxon project, provides inservice sessions on long-term planning, implementing math menus, investigating the math strands, and reinventing traditional algorithms.

Demonstration

Just as children need to see readers and writers using literacy and mathematics in the real world, so teachers need to see other teachers modeling and demonstrating new strategies and techniques. Talking and reading aren't enough. Teachers need to observe and interact with articulate professionals who are using the strategies they are hoping to learn.

A great many principals are excellent teachers, are trusted and respected by their staff, and are able to demonstrate new strategies with students. But no matter how wonderful a principal may be, teachers still tend to trust the ability of other teachers who work with "their kind of kids" every day.

At best, any outsider (including the principal) coming into a classroom can only demonstrate a "canned" lesson that has been successful with other classes. I am very much a part of my school's learning community, but I can never respond to a classroom of students as authentically as their classroom teacher, who knows each student individually and who has also examined the social nature of that specific grouping. Teachers recognize this fact of life as well. Staff members need to see "regular" teachers dealing with real students in everyday settings.

It is crucial for a principal to highlight the strengths of his teachers. Many times outside "experts" are seen as having some magical advantage over the rest of the world, and this is simply not the case. It sends a powerful message to our teacher colleagues when we take the time to observe them engaged in their craft and hail them as people with ideas and instructional practices from which their colleagues can learn.

I want each of my teachers to become an "expert" in some area of the math curriculum, and here are some specific ways I start them down that road:

- Through my conversations with them and my observations in their classroom, I help teachers identify their curricular strengths and encourage them to collaborate with one another.

- I encourage them to volunteer for district committees, offering to accompany them if that will make them feel more comfortable.

- I encourage them to share their expertise with staff members through mini–inservice presentations at staff meetings or workshops.

- I invite them to copresent with me or with peers at district and local conferences.

- I arrange to cover their classrooms so they can attend special events/conferences, observe in a colleague's classroom, or observe a teacher in another school.

- I encourage them to invite other teachers to observe in their classroom.

- I point out specific strengths in each classroom whenever I give visitors tours of the school.

- I write about teachers' work in the school newsletter and acknowledge that work at PTA and other parent gatherings.

I also believe that learning is more meaningful and powerful in social contexts. We learn more together than we can by ourselves. And I don't always have to be the one who facilitates and directs observations (although that is certainly an important part of my job). The presence of another colleague invites discussion, reflection, and further discussion. Teachers think more deeply when they are able to discuss their reflections with a colleague. I encourage my teachers to observe and to attend workshops and conferences in pairs and small groups.

Engagement

Reading a few books and articles and encountering some new strategies doesn't ensure learning. Teachers need to grapple with the things they read and the strategies they encounter, both internally and in discussions with their peers. New ideas need to be thought about in many contexts, reflected on, talked about. You can teach something till the cows come home, but if the learners don't tune in, they aren't learning.

So when does all this thinking and talking take place? Time is the teacher's greatest and most precious resource. After-school meetings are always an option, but teachers are exhausted at the end of the day, and they have personal lives as well. Here are a few strategies for helping two, three, or four teachers find an hour or two to observe, plan, discuss, or study.

- Show a film in the library or cafeteria to two classes at a time and follow up with a simple math extension activity.

- Persuade, cajole, or strong-arm district administrators and curriculum developers to be guest teachers once in while.

- If your school doesn't have a strict transportation timetable, extend the school day fifteen minutes a day for four days each week; then dismiss classes an hour earlier one day a week and use the hour for staff development.

- Extend student lunch times an additional half hour occasionally to give teachers time for a working lunch.

- Ask the school support staff (custodians, nurses, cooks and food servers, monitors, crossing guards, counselors) to discuss issues related to their jobs with groups of students. (I generally offer to be present and often use a meeting like this as an opportunity to problem-solve.)

Expectation

New learning stretches our limits; we find ourselves in disequilibrium. There has to be a general expectation for success on the part of the teachers (and on your part as evaluator).

Teachers need to trust that you view them as smart and capable, because sometimes their confidence will be shaken. They have to visualize themselves in the role expected of them before they will be comfortable in their learning. It is your job to maintain high but reasonable expectations for professional growth in individual teachers. Teachers will rise to the occasion if they feel you trust their judgment and will be there to support them if things don't go well.

Responsibility

Teachers need to see themselves as responsible for their own learning. Otherwise the accountability for change will always remain with the evaluator or those who are forcing the change. I cannot make teachers learn any new concept or strategy unless they have decided that the new idea is worthwhile and they are willing to risk moving into disequilibrium.

A principal is in the position to focus teachers on their role as reflective practitioners and push their thinking. He does this through conversation, not interrogation. Putting teachers on the defensive by asking why they aren't using a particular practice will never create an environment of professional trust. Rather, teachers should be continually reminded of their responsibility to be deliberate in their decision making.

Every October, I invite teachers in for an annual "talkover." During our hour together, we very briefly discuss each student in the class as a learner. I take notes and keep track of those children about whom the teacher has concerns so that support staff and I can keep an eye on these children. I also review the curricular goals set by the teacher in our May evaluation conference and find out whether the teacher still feels committed to those goals. Since mathematics has been our major curricular goal for several years, I also ask teachers to identify specific mathematics areas in which they feel they need to grow. We then discuss how I can support them as learners in meeting their goals.

Use

Learners don't get ready to learn; they are constantly learning. Teachers can read, discuss, and observe all they want, but new knowledge can take hold only when it is being used. Teachers have to be given the permission to risk teaching outside their comfort zone. They won't try new strategies unless they feel supported in their efforts. Principals must reflect on their role as evaluators and be prepared to support teachers in their efforts to change.

Each week I read a children's book in every classroom so that students and teachers can see me in an instructional context and so that I am continually reminded of the daily challenges faced by classroom teachers. In keeping with our "literature and mathematics" focus, I almost always choose children's literature that will spark a mathematical discussion or extension activity. I often leave children with a question *(How many of me would it take to make a tyrannosaurus if I am six feet tall?)* and ask them to share their thinking with me by way of the schoolwide postal system.

Approximation

When we try out new ideas and practices, we must never expect to get it right the first time. We have our professional and instructional goals in mind, but we have to reflect on our attempts as approximations, not failures. A principal should be a cheerleader, supporting the approximations of staff members in their attempts to make significant changes in their practice.

When teachers instigate new practices and strategies, they must first focus on what went well, then on what can be done differently. Evaluation must be goal oriented; teachers need to reflect on their growth and be more deliberate in their decision making. Principals must find ways to help teachers reflect on their strengths and risk identifying areas in need of growth.

Each teacher is different in terms of how much disequilibrium can be tolerated at any given time and in any given curricular area. I like to think about change using the metaphor of a swimming pool: Some people are willing to dive right in over their head at the beginning but come up quickly near the edge for security. Some people have to wade in slowly, testing the water every step of the way. Some need to hang on to an inflated ball or tube before they feel safe enough to leave the edge. Some won't get into the pool until they see all the fun that others are having. And some have such overriding hydrophobia that it takes a great deal of coaxing and counseling for them even to get near the pool.

Each staff member is different in her or his comfort level for change. If I acknowledge only the divers, then I will never get the waders in past their knees (certainly not past their navels!). And even the divers need some security to hold on to as they plunge into water over their heads. I have to get some people in the pool to model for the others that their efforts will be worthwhile. And if the pool is too cold or perceived as being full of alligators, or if the swimmers are being dunked too often, nobody wants to stay in the water.

Response

A principal has more control over this condition of learning than any of the others. Nobody can control what another person does or says. But everyone should be in control of their response to other people. Principals, in the way they respond to attempts at change, hold the power to nurture or kill the spirit of a faculty. Principals must first see themselves as learners before they can begin to take on the role of change agents. Only when you see yourself as a learner will you appreciate the efforts and risks taken by others.

4

Requirements for Change

Judith L. Rosen

Judith Rosen has been an elementary school principal for fourteen years and is currently the principal of Jefferson Elementary School, in the Sunset section of San Francisco. The school enjoys an excellent reputation both within and beyond the neighborhood. The Jefferson student body, kindergarten though fifth grade, comprises 530 children. Twenty-eight percent of the students are white, 45 percent are Chinese, and 27 percent are other nonwhite races, which is consistent with the demographics of the area. Thirty-five percent of the students receive a free or reduced-price lunch.

t is interesting, as well as perplexing, to reflect on change and how it comes about. It can be difficult to see the big picture, because you usually end up going in a somewhat different direction from the one in which you originally started out. But I can point to three major requirements for change, which comprise any number of lesser ones.

First, if change is going to take place, a leader must have a vision of what she wants and be able to communicate that vision to her school community. Second, the means to accomplish this vision must be broken down into small, clearly understood steps in which everyone participates collaboratively and congenially—no top-down mandates allowed. Third, professional development is crucial; teachers need to understand the new curriculum.

In fulfilling these requirements, one must recognize that real change, systemic change, comes about over many years; it cannot be accomplished quickly. Changing the way we teach mathematics at Jefferson took more than seven years. Some years much was accomplished, others not so much. But we never stopped moving completely, and there were no major setbacks.

A Bit of History

Before coming to Jefferson, I had been a principal for three years at another school. My first year there I made no changes:

I followed existing school policy, the faculty and staff were very cooperative and supportive, and everything ran smoothly and efficiently. I assumed that if the school provided discipline, safety, and order—if everyone knew and understood the rules—the students would learn. Sure, I visited classrooms and supported the curriculum, but I wasn't really involved in the academic side of things.

The second year, I started redefining my role. Was I a manager or a curriculum leader? Could I—or anyone—be both? It is certainly very important for a school to operate smoothly and efficiently, but too often administrators—and teachers, as well—get mired in their managerial role and forget the real goal, which is educating children. The ultimate focus must be on curriculum if we, the school community, are truly going to teach our children to become bright, articulate, contributing members of society. I decided that to be an instructional leader, I needed to immerse myself in curriculum. I began reading educational journals and articles that spoke about curriculum. I also enrolled in a three-year leadership training program.

The third year, now realizing how important it is to grow professionally, to encounter new ideas about curriculum and how children learn, I started sharing what I was learning and reading with the faculty. I also made sure teachers had professional development opportunities of their own. I made some inroads, but they were small. I knew I needed to be more forceful and direct in stating my vision. But by the end of that year, my philosophy had been articulated: I wanted to educate the whole child, heart as well as mind. To that end, I knew an important part of my leadership would center on providing professional development opportunities to teachers.

Planting the Seed

I became the principal of Jefferson in 1988. The school had an excellent reputation academically. Teachers taught traditional textbook mathematics using traditional methods. The Mathematics Framework for California Public Schools, released the year before, was not yet being embraced at Jefferson, or at any other school in San Francisco, for that matter, except in a few individual classrooms.

I saw this as an opportunity to help students become real learners instead of simply parroting back answers on Friday tests. In my experience, students rarely seemed inquisitive or engaged; they did what their teacher told them, completing work that placed little emphasis on creativity and variety. Children were learning, yes, but their learning could be so much richer and more meaningful. As a staff, we needed to learn a variety of teaching strategies so that we could meet the needs of *all* students. We needed to look at our teaching practices and figure out what worked and how to change what didn't work.

I decided to focus specifically on the math curriculum for several reasons. First, the California mathematics framework was a hot topic. Second, I was very interested in the many articles that were being written about teaching and understanding mathematics in this new way. Third, through the leadership training program I was enrolled in, I was well connected with other educators in the school district who were excited about the framework. Finally, two teachers at Jefferson had taken a math leadership course at San Francisco State University and were committed to this kind of student learning.

My goal was to familiarize the teachers with the framework and get them to implement it in our classrooms so that our students could become mathematical thinkers. I knew it would be difficult. There was no textbook, there were few materials, and there wasn't much information about how to teach according to this new philosophy.

During my early months at Jefferson, I noticed some hesitancy on the part of some of the teachers when I spoke about the California mathematics framework, which I did quite frequently at faculty and grade-level meetings. There was no outright opposition, but I could tell the framework was not really understood and there was little interest in implementing it in the classroom. The feeling seemed to be, *We're fine, why are*

*you asking us to change? Our test scores are good, our parents
and children are happy, so leave us alone.*

But five teachers out of seventeen were willing to listen
and seemed to embrace my curriculum vision, namely that we
need to change our teaching so that children can have opportunities to expand their thinking and knowledge. In the lunch-
room one day, while a group of us were talking about change,
one teacher, to whom I will be forever grateful, said, "You
know, I don't want to go to a doctor who practices medicine
exactly the same way he did twenty years ago. Medicine has
changed!" That was a defining moment: it said, yes, we need
to make changes, not for the sake of change, but for the better-
ment of our children and ourselves. This was the kind of thing
I needed to hear.

That year two of my teachers and I attended the Northern California Math Conference. I was extremely impressed,
most of all by the dedication and excitement of the participants. These teachers and administrators had given up their
weekend in order to learn. The professionalism that perme-
ated the conference was invigorating. I came away refreshed,
renewed, and heartened. I vowed to attend the conference
every year and to encourage my teachers and colleagues to attend as well. At our next faculty meeting, I spoke eagerly of my
joy at seeing teachers learning together with such fervor and
commitment.

By spring I was determined to make some recognizable progress toward implementing the math framework in the classroom. Knowing that it was essential for teachers to understand the framework, I scheduled a number of faculty-meeting presentations, led by a teacher on my faculty and by a friend of mine who teaches at another school. Always, I encouraged teachers to try new ideas and approaches, to share what they were reading in educational journals. I also convinced seven of my teachers to apply for a team grant of $5,000 to support implementing the framework. The money would pay for math manipulatives and replacement units and would offset a portion of the cost of attending the Northern California Math Conference. They were awarded the grant in May, and we agreed to meet monthly in the coming year to assess our progress. I appreciated the boost the money would give our efforts, of course, but I was even more pleased that seven teachers had joined together in a common goal. Working together was important.

As the year ended, I felt change was beginning to happen. The seven team teachers were committed to implementing the math framework. The two new teachers I hired to replace teachers who were retiring had taken the math leadership course at San Francisco State and were also committed to implementing the framework. I knew that we could now have meaningful conversations centered around the school's new philosophy: a commitment to educating the whole child, heart and mind; a commitment to implementing the California math framework; and a commitment to staff development.

At this point I felt I needed to become very familiar with the framework and with the NCTM *Curriculum and Evaluation Standards for School Mathematics* (1989). That summer I began to read as much as I could. I wanted to be able to be a resource for the staff, and I also wanted to encourage them to become more involved in their professional development. I would be supportive of and involved in what they were doing in math but also as it related to other areas of the curriculum.

Helping It Grow

My second year at Jefferson was a breakthrough year. When I returned in the fall, another teacher retired and I hired Lynne Zolli, who was very committed to the school's philosophy. Bonnie Tank, a Marilyn Burns Education Associates math consultant, had met Lynne the year before and called me to ask whether she could work with Lynne in her classroom. I was delighted, and immediately said yes. Bonnie's presence at Jefferson would further our understanding of how mathematics should be taught.

With money from our math grant, we were able to purchase math manipulatives and professional books. I made sure to share our "math news" with the other teachers and with parents—in our newsletters and teacher bulletins, at PTA meetings and faculty meetings. I wanted everyone to know about the changes being brought about as a result of the California math framework.

When I visited the classrooms in which mathematics was being taught according to the framework, I found children taking part in meaningful activities, often working in pairs to solve problems. I looked on as students were encouraged to suggest different ways of solving a problem. I encountered children unafraid to explain the thinking that led them to their answer. It was heartening to see children free to hypothesize, to figure out that you could add up for a subtraction problem.

During the year I continued to distribute journal articles that dealt with what we were trying to do in mathematics. Dr. Carol Langbort, a professor at San Francisco State University, spoke to the teachers about the math leadership course, again being offered the following summer, and she made a number of repeat visits during the year, visiting each math framework classroom individually. Seeing how much she cared, how interested she was in what was really happening in the trenches, was a tremendous validation for the teachers working so hard to teach mathematics in a meaningful and thinking context. They, and I, were extremely proud and pleased.

Bearing Fruit

In May, 1992, the California State Department of Education re-leased a revision of the mathematics framework. The document addressed the philosophy behind the vision I had for the school and validated the kind of teaching and learning I had been talking about since my arrival. It was important for teachers, and parents, to see this in print. It was an exciting time! Math educators everywhere were enthusiastic about the direction math instruction was taking, not only in California but throughout the country. As Marilyn Burns said in her speech at the Northern California Math Conference in December, 1989, we were going to enable children to become "mathematical thinkers instead of just mathematical doers."

Four of our teachers attended the Northern California Math Conference that year. Bonnie Tank was also with us again, partly funded through a grant from Exxon Corporation. She was working on a book about probability, using Patrick Mulkeen's second-grade classroom as her laboratory. In April Bonnie suggested applying for a grant from Exxon's Math K–3 Project to bring her to Jefferson as a math consultant to work with teachers as they implemented the California math framework. What a boost this would be if we were fortunate enough to get it!

Since our intention was to include the whole school, I felt I needed the commitment of the entire staff. With Bonnie's help, I immediately set to work, meeting with a representative group of teachers to put together our proposal. In May we submitted an application setting forth a four-pronged plan for using the money:

1. Contracting with Bonnie for a total of forty days over the coming school year, during which time she would work with teachers in their classrooms, lead inservice sessions, and (very important) talk with parents at PTA meetings.

2. Hiring substitutes so that teachers could be released from their classrooms for daylong grade-level meetings.

3. Purchasing materials.

4. Paying fees for teachers to attend workshops/conferences.

Being awarded the grant in August was heartening and very gratifying. A large corporation valued what we were trying to accomplish and was willing to give us real money to see whether we could indeed create systemic change. Even better, the administrators of the program under which the grant was awarded realized this was a long-term project, not something that was going to happen quickly. They had validated our slow beginnings and our steady pace toward change. This was it, the real turning point in the way we were going to teach mathematics! I was thrilled for myself, for the teachers, and most of all for the children.

In September, I eagerly told the larger school community about the grant and how it would be used to change our math program. I knew some of our teachers were still concerned about this new direction, that many parents were worried about the philosophy behind it. Convinced that parental support was essential, the teachers and I were cautious and careful about how we told parents about the program: we wanted them to understand fully what we were doing. We assured them that we wanted their children to learn their basic facts, but we emphasized that students needed to become mathematical thinkers, not just mathematical doers.

Good things continued to happen. During the next few years many math "menus," replacement units, and professional books hit the market. The Exxon grant provided money for us to purchase these materials and train our teachers in how to use them. We were able to institutionalize collaboration and collegiality. Teachers could sustain the changes they were making in their teaching, support one another, work with specialists.

Looking Back

Many factors enter into any story of change. It comes about by having a clear vision of what you want, being able to communicate that vision, always finding ways to pursue the vision, not getting sidetracked. You also need to go slowly: small steady steps lead to big steps. It is important to honor people's accomplishments, to encourage and support the teachers who are willing to be part of the change and give them integral roles in effecting it.

It is equally important not to alienate people: the one thing you don't want to do is divide the school community into camps. Everyone must be invited to the table. (At the same time, you cannot allow roadblocks or sabotage: with majority support, policies can be enforced.) Always capitalize on the good things that happen. Validate your vision: circulate newspaper stories, journal articles, books. Share the good ideas you encounter at conferences and workshops, and encourage the entire school community to do the same. When you ask for staff, community, or student input, be sure you really want it—and then listen to their suggestions and opinions and take them into consideration.

Monetary grants are clearly another very important piece of the process. It costs money to grow professionally. In addition, the collaboration required to apply for and use grant money fosters teamwork and unity in the school community. (Every year at Jefferson, teachers have applied for and received grants, ranging from individual grants of $2,000 to team grants of $5,000.)

Another significant factor is being able to hire eager teachers whose philosophy is compatible with new methods and ideas. New blood can be crucial. Jefferson has been fortunate in this regard. Over the past eleven years, ten teachers have retired, two have left the area, and one has accepted a special assignment. I have drawn up a list of questions that I ask each candidate for each new position, and I share these questions with the entire staff. Everyone knows what I expect in a teacher.

What it all comes down to, finally, is that you can't do it alone. Looking back on my experience at Jefferson, I happily admit how extremely fortunate I am to be surrounded by outstanding teachers who are committed to student learning and to their own professional growth. With the leadership of organizations like the National Council of Teachers of Mathematics, the National Science Foundation, and the Exxon Corporation, we have come a long way in looking at how children learn and in recognizing how important the teaching strategies we use are. The culture of education today resonates with a positive and productive attitude toward student learning.

5

Toward a Quality Math Program: A Principal's Principles

Rosanna Gallagher

Rosanna Gallagher, principal of Robins Elementary School, in the Tucson (Arizona) Unified School District, was named Arizona's Distinguished Principal of 1999. Robins Elementary is five years old and is located in a densely populated urban area. The student body of 360 is made up of 45 percent minority children and 55 percent European American children. The school's curricular and extracurricular program is based on current educational research and practice.

A principal's role in restructuring math learning is to help her teachers create classrooms in which mathematical inquiry and success are encouraged and supported. As the teacher sets the tone for learning in the classroom, the principal sets the tone for learning in the larger school community.

Looking back at our personal and professional life, we are able to identify certain defining moments, moments of encouragement and validation. One of mine is sitting in front of a small television set in the Cuisenaire booth at an NCTM conference, watching a videotape from the series *Mathematics: Teaching for Understanding* (Marilyn Burns, Cuisenaire, 1992). I was the principal of the school featured on the tape, Drachman Primary Magnet School, a small urban primary school in the Tucson (Arizona) Unified School District. Our minority enrollment was extremely high, and many of our students lived in government housing projects; violence and welfare were part of their lives. A few short years before, the school's district test scores had ranked at the very bottom. Now our students and teachers were serving as models for educators all over the country.

As someone who is forever learning, I am also gratified by the effort and collaboration undertaken at my current school over the past several years, hard work that has resulted in ever better math scores on national standardized tests. I believe our experience reveals some fundamental principles for the principal interested in providing authentic and meaningful instruction—in math, especially, but also in all learning. These principles are followed by all good leaders; ideally, they should be understood and supported by every member of your school community—teachers, parents, and students alike.

Principle No. 1

Provide professional growth opportunities that build the best learning environment for your students, their parents, the teachers, and staff.

In his book *On Becoming a Leader* (Addison-Wesley, 1994), Warren Bennis quotes Piaget as saying, "Every time we teach a child something, we keep him from inventing himself." Bennis then goes Piaget one better: "Every time we teach a child something, rather than helping him to learn, we keep him from inventing himself. By its very nature, teaching homogenizes, both its subjects and its objects. *Learning*, on the other hand, liberates. The more we know about ourselves and our world, the freer we are to achieve everything we are capable of achieving" (p. 69).

Focusing on being a facilitator of learning rather than a purveyor of information profoundly affects the decisions we make. *What* we teach in math has been made clear through NCTM standards and state and district core curriculum performance objectives. These are the tools or skills that our students will use in the process of learning. However, *how* and *why* we teach math is where we put Bennis's statement into practice.

A school's direction and environment will reflect the goals and understanding of its decision makers. You cannot facilitate or support math learning for others if you do not have a foundation in or an understanding of mathematical concepts and the learning process in general. This is true for administrators, teachers, students, and parents, and therefore math learning opportunities at all levels and for many different purposes must be a vital part of any professional development program. To be able to help select the appropriate resources and topics, you must make every effort to remain as knowledgeable and current as possible.

The principal's role in staff development is fivefold:

1. Determine, based on individual and collective interest and on identified needs, the areas in which development is necessary.

2. Identify specific avenues and programs (district math in-service programs, site-based math workshops/study groups, math courses) that will provide the appropriate opportunities.

3. Find the necessary funding.

4. Find and/or support ways for teachers to participate in ongoing math discussions with other teachers, their students, and their students' parents. The value of teaching others about a new discovery is immeasurable.

5. Encourage teachers to take part in outreach presentations at district, state, and national conferences.

We must also help parents understand that the approaches we are using to develop math proficiency are more meaningful than relying solely on textbooks, workbooks, timed tests, and the other skill-and-drill methods they experienced as part of their own schooling. Parent education continues to be one of my greatest challenges, and here are some ways I've tried to accomplish it:

• Scheduling "math curriculum nights" featuring commercial videotapes, guest speakers, and/or student-led demonstrations and workshops.

- Conducting individual meetings/classroom visits to show parents how specific activities are being used to teach math skills.

- Setting up a school leadership team made up of teachers and parents to investigate additional opportunities for parents to better understand and support the way their child is learning math in school and to recommend ways for parents to support their child's math growth outside school.

Principle No. 2

Model and support being a learner and risk taker.

We all know teachers who have spent their entire career in the same room in the same building and who put up the same bulletin board, use the same lesson plans, and assign the same worksheets year after year. We've lamented the teachers who won't budge from their desk, who refuse to attend inservice workshops or, if they do attend, never try any of the new teaching ideas they encounter there.

Unfortunately, administrators all too often slip smoothly into this same mold. For effective change to take place in the classroom, administrators must *model* the changes they want to see. The admonition *Do as I say and not as I do!* will not produce a successful learning environment. When I was a new principal, I had the privilege of participating in a Title I math staff development program that helped me see how administrators play an invaluable role in encouraging teachers to continue to learn and to use their newfound knowledge to change their classroom practice. I continue to participate in as many of our school staff development activities as possible because:

- It shows that I support the particular area of study.

- I can better support the implementation of this new knowledge in the classroom if I understand it.

I often tell teachers that we cannot ask students to do what we are not willing to do ourselves, and this principle holds true for administrators as well—we cannot ask teachers to be lifelong learners if we are not modeling being a learner ourselves.

Since risk taking is a fundamental part of being a learner, administrators must also take risks and, yes, be willing to make mistakes! Some of my greatest opportunities to model being a learner have been how I react to mistakes that I or others have made. Without mistakes, there is little opportunity to learn. Instead, we have students who will not write words they cannot spell, will not try to solve a mathematical problem, will not share their thinking. We have teachers who will not try a new teaching approach, parents who are unwilling to support a different way of learning, administrators who will not or cannot support an exciting new program.

Although I had a strong curriculum background when I became a principal, I readily admit that math is not one of my strong suits. This opens up great opportunities for personal and professional growth and risk taking. Often I team teach with someone in the early stages of restructuring her approach to math. As partners in planning and executing classroom activities, we experience firsthand how difficult it is to allow children to come to their own mathematical conclusions. The teacher sees that I am also learning and have many of the same questions about how to become a facilitator of learning instead of a provider of information. Together we wean ourselves from worksheets and textbooks and strive to provide more authentic experiences that teach and reinforce basic math skills and at the same time help students understand and connect math concepts. Our common experience allows us to talk about—and work through—the risky business of shifting the way we view math education.

Based on my experience and observations, I've identified behavior indicating that a principal is modeling and supporting risk taking and learning:

Risk taking and learning are being modeled when:

- The principal attends math classes, inservice programs, study groups, etc.

- The principal shares new math learning by making presentations at inservice programs, district meetings, conferences, etc.

- The principal tries new math knowledge/ strategies with students and others.

- The principal tries his own math ideas in the classroom.

- The principal is comfortable learning from others in the school community.

Risk taking and learning are being supported when:

- Teachers are encouraged and helped to attend math classes, workshops, etc.

- Teachers/students/parents are encouraged to share new math knowledge with others through presentations, conferences, etc.

- Teachers/students/parents are encouraged, supported, and recognized for using new math knowledge.

- Teachers/students/parents are encouraged to try their own creative math ideas.

- Teachers/students/parents are respected for their areas of expertise and encouraged to express their ideas and opinions.

- The principal knows where she is as a learner and seeks resources, classes, and learning opportunities for her own growth in math.

- The principal knows where teachers, students, and parents are as learners and supports their individual growth in math.

- The principal is comfortable making mistakes.

- The principal understands when others make mistakes.

- The principal becomes a co–teacher/learner with teachers, students, and parents.

- The principal supports and encourages team teaching/planning for math instruction.

Principle No. 3

Foster a team approach.

Math instruction benefits greatly from a team approach. Collaborative problem solving lies at the foundation of current math education. Students are encouraged to share their approaches to solving a problem, think of additional ways to solve the problem, apply their math knowledge and experience to new situations, and respect and learn from one another. The classroom teacher who gives his students opportunities to pose questions, explore mathematical solutions individually and collaboratively, and share the results is building a team.

Math instruction developed by a team of teachers and administrators works the same way. Staff members share questions, concerns, research, information, and goals. They communicate their knowledge, experience, and thinking with one another through study groups, team meetings, teacher-led inservice sessions, parent workshops. They encounter and evaluate many different ideas and approaches to problem solving and curriculum. The math abilities of all participants improve, and the team is stronger and more able to provide successful and meaningful learning opportunities.

But we must remember that building an effective team takes time. Learning, working, and practicing together is a gradual process. Many school faculties and administrations with all the ingredients for success in place, like sports squads with great natural ability, have never reached their full potential because they haven't taken the time to build the team. Individual learning and growth may produce an outstanding student, parent, teacher, or classroom, but the power of a successful school community is unleashed when everyone contributes his or her individual strengths to the team. A teacher who implements an outstanding math program in her classroom must be encouraged and helped to strengthen the math program in other classrooms. Individual accomplishments should always be recognized, of course, but working to raise the level of an entire program is the ultimate achievement. At our school, for example, a respected math teacher formed a biweekly study group that 75 percent of the teaching staff voluntarily attended all year. Our math program and the entire school community were strengthened.

Principle No. 4

Respect and honor the key role of the classroom teacher and the classroom environment.

"Despite reports of national commissions, despite state mandates, and despite carefully engineered and expertly driven change strategies, it is the 2.2 million teachers that account for 26 billion teacher-contact hours in schools across the nation that will in the end decide what happens to students" (T. J. Sergiovanni, *Leadership for the Schoolhouse*, Jossey-Bass, 1966, p. 156).

Improvement in math instruction will not happen at any level without the involvement of the classroom teacher. How teachers are treated as persons and professionals has a tremendous influence on how they treat their students and affects the attitude with which they approach their classroom program. At a minimum, teachers should participate in any decision that involves schoolwide math programs, materials, and professional development. Their direct daily contact with students is an obvious reason to respect the enormous influence they have on student learning and on how students feel about themselves as learners.

But we must do more than respect the role of the classroom teacher; we must *honor* that role. In honoring someone, we go out of our way to listen when she speaks, and we respond to her thoughtfully. We point out all the great things he makes possible, we are in awe of her accomplishments. We are grateful to have a part in helping him continue his success, we are proud of our association with her. Being valued in this way, teachers in turn honor the students in their care.

The success of a program in math or any other area depends on whether teachers feel their own classroom practices are successful. Schoolwide math instruction can improve only to the degree that every classroom teacher is involved in the change. Truly, the success of a principal's leadership and the school's academic programs will be measured by the success of all members of the learning community.

Principle No. 5

Develop a how-can-I-help-you-do-that frame of mind.

One of my favorite books on leadership is *The Art of Supportive Leadership,* by J. Donald Walters (Crystal Clarity, 1993). His definition of leadership is this: "Genuine leadership is of only one type: *supportive*. It leads people: It doesn't drive them. It involves them: It doesn't coerce them. It never loses sight of the most important principle governing any project involving human beings: namely, that people are more important than things" (p. 11).

Thinking back on the changes in math instruction I have supported over the years, I realize that my greatest contribution to that change has simply been to help others do the things they want to do, realize the ideas they think are important. Helping a teacher get the materials she needs, supporting a teacher's desire to teach math through music, finding a way for a team to attend a math conference, listening to the first hesitant formulations of new ideas, I support math change by supporting those who must implement the changes—the teachers.

In my work as a principal, I've often thought to myself, *Wouldn't it be great if I called the district office with this idea and they said, How can I help you do it?* The times this has happened have resulted in some of the best professional experiences of my career. The underlying message in this response is that I am trusted and supported as a person and a professional. Knowing that I have this kind of support not only gives me confidence but helps me commit to making my idea successful. Teachers, parents, and students need this same kind of response.

While some ideas are not feasible, many are and can be supported quite easily. Saying *Tell me more about it* lets me see the thought and planning that have gone into the idea. Knowing that, I can better offer my support, whether by saying *Go ahead,* by offering assistance, or by finding funding. An investment like this pays great dividends in bringing about true change and program growth. An idea that is owned and supported pushes instruction to a higher level.

Many ideas from students, teachers, and parents have resulted in improving math instruction in our school. The math study group I mentioned earlier is one: through it we looked at math as part of our entire curriculum and began to define how an environment that supports math learning should look. Now when I go into classrooms and see students applying math concepts using a variety of materials and strategies, hear them discussing their learning and perspectives, I know emphatically that we have come a long way from the direct instruction of rules and worksheets.

Kids-Teaching-Kids Day, an idea a group of students brought to me, is another powerful activity that has become a permanent part of our program. Students plan mini-workshops, which other students sign up to take. A recent KTK Day focused on math: students had to connect their workshop to math learning. As I read the lesson plans and observed the workshops, I was amazed at the impact this program has had on student learning. Students all over the school were teaching and learning math in the context of cooking, weaving, and flying paper airplanes.

Principle No. 6

Define your role as principal based on the needs of the program.

One of the fundamental characteristics of successful leadership is to have a firm vision for the school's progress. I would amend this by adding that a leader *in a growing and changing organization* must have a *flexible* vision. Someone once asked me how I "knew" what to do to bring about change in our school program. I answered that any success I may have had is because I don't have an agenda to impose but rather base my role on the specific needs of the program.

While there are some fundamental principles that all leaders apply (principles I am sharing in this essay), my role with regard to a particular program or idea depends on where the team is in the process. Over time that role can go from being the pivotal instigator of change to supporting the widening number of stakeholders in the school community who have embraced that change.

In the beginning stages of change I need to make a variety of resources available that will help team members acquire the knowledge they need to be able to build a solid math program. As team members become more confident, my role shifts to supporting *their* ideas and requests. Eventually the school becomes a partnership in which the various members, all of them at different but equal levels, lead and support one another's growth. As the program reaches subsequent levels of success, I concentrate on finding ways to keep everyone excited and challenged. This cycle, or pattern, repeats itself, to different degrees, again and again in any healthy school environment.

Whether your school is just beginning to develop a new math program or already has one well under way, you must be able to adjust your leadership to fit its current status and provide what it needs to continue. Most programs have many strands of growth going on simultaneously, and individuals within each strand are at different points in the cycle. While I am very proud of our math program, I am very aware of the different needs of various teachers, aides, students, and parents; I know that how I help meet those needs will play an important role in the continued growth of our program. One of the true challenges of being a principal today is continually redefining your role based on the cycle of change. Being able to do so defines you as a leader.

Principle No. 7

Believe that anything is possible.

Perhaps the best part of a principal's job is celebrating the realization of impossible dreams. My own most recent such celebration occurred when a team of teachers from our school fulfilled their dream of giving a presentation at the national NCTM conference, in Washington, D.C. We had been invited to share the story of our school's revitalized math program, and we needed to raise thousands of dollars to pay for the trip. We also needed to find a way for 70 percent of our classroom teachers to be away from school the same week!

Wonderful and creative staff members, among them our special education teachers, guidance counselor, and librarian, volunteered to fill in for their colleagues. Our district assistant superintendent helped us negotiate the maze of district regulations and requirements. Parents and students organized a schoolwide "mathathon" to raise money both for the trip and for teachers to spend on math materials at the conference. When a grant from Exxon provided the remaining money we needed, we packed our bags.

Our presentation contained a number of components:

- The Art of Balancing Mathematics, by Sandy Kaser (intermediate-multiage teacher). Incorporating math in art through investigations of the work of Alexander Calder and Aristotle's principles of balance.

- The Recipe for Mathematical Inquiry, by Judi Busche (intermediate-multiage teacher). Using patterns and cooking to encourage students to make their own math learning connections.

- Pushing the Math Button, by Grace Rendes and Tina Castro (kindergarten team-teachers). Using buttons to teach mathematical concepts and skills.

- Measuring Fractions Through Music, by Lori Fraesdorf (third-grade teacher). Helping students understand fractions through musical notation.

- Growing Mathematics, by Leslie Kahn (intermediate-multiage teacher). Learning about area and perimeter and exploring patterns via a garden project.

- Fully Including Math, by Carol Martin and Elsa Fimbres (primary-multiage team-teachers). Modifying math learning for a special-needs student who is part of a regular classroom.

Together we had taken the first steps toward change and were now seeing math connections everywhere. Our exchange of new ideas, thoughts, and experiences had become the basis for educational reform. These educators were bringing tremendous opportunities to their students—clearly reason to celebrate.

6

Mathematics Reform:
One District's Story

Arthur Camins and Sheldon Berman

Sheldon Berman became superintendent of the Hudson (Massachusetts) Public Schools in 1993, at a time when dramatic cutbacks in funding to education had undermined morale in the district. To achieve his vision of active, inquiry-based learning, he needed to rebuild the district's financial base, foster a common understanding of education goals and methods, encourage leadership and initiative on the part of teachers, and provide teachers with resources and professional development. Money obtained through the Massachusetts Education Reform Act and other grants in support of mathematics and science reform enabled him to move this agenda forward. In the summer of 1997 he hired Arthur Camins as the district's first full-time elementary mathematics and science director. (Up to that time there had been no full-time or part-time curriculum coordination.) This is the story of how Camins, Berman, and others worked together to bring about mathematics and science reform.

Reform is driven primarily by a vision of the goals and content of education, a deep understanding of the complexity of systemic change, and the passion and persistence to see the struggle through. The starting point is always what we want for young people—what kind of people we want them to be.

In Hudson, as in school districts everywhere, we want to enable young people to develop the knowledge, skills, and habits of mind to be able to recognize and discover patterns in the natural and social world and make reasoned judgments based on evidence. Our goal is to enable them to make sense of their world and to be fully informed participants in decision making. Mathematics education, as a disciplined pattern-seeking enterprise, is uniquely suited to fulfilling this challenge.

A New View of Mathematics Education

In traditional mathematics programs, even those with hands-on components, students are typically introduced to algorithmic strategies, asked to practice these computations, and then given problems to which these strategies can be applied. In a guided-inquiry approach to mathematics instruction, children investigate phenomena or problems and devise multiple problem-solving strategies as well as stunning facility in expressing their mathematical thinking.

Promoting systemic reform that realizes this vision of mathematics education requires that a district provide multiple entry points and take into account teachers' varying interests and different rates of development. Just as effective classroom instruction begins with student preconceptions, strategies for professional development and systemic reform must take into account teacher ideas and experiences. Our challenge has been to advance a vision of children's active engagement in building numeracy while meeting the developmental needs of the teachers who will make that engagement come alive.

To meet this challenge, students, teachers, building and district administrators, parents, and school board members must unite on a transformative journey. To develop a new view of mathematics education for all students, reform must be both systemwide and systemic. Hudson is in the middle of this journey. Although we are seeing significant changes in instruction and student performance, implementing systemwide change is a continuing challenge.

The Context

Hudson is a low- to middle-income district of 2,750 students with a significant bilingual population. Beginning in 1990, the area economy experienced a significant decline, producing large-scale cuts of staff and programs. Professional development was all but eliminated. On the whole the faculty was an experienced and solid group of teachers, interested in innovation in mathematics yet cut off from the resources to pursue change.

In addition, the district did not have a consistent curriculum across grade levels. Although there were curriculum guidelines, they often remained hidden in teachers' desks. Each school determined its own textbooks and instructional materials, and these were at times even inconsistent within the school. Teachers were semiautonomous, the key architects of their own instructional program. Although this was empowering to them personally, the lack of consistency across grades and schools was frustrating. It also affected student achievement: in the standardized state assessments in mathematics, the district scored quite low compared with surrounding communities. Most faculty members felt that if the district's curriculum was unified, they would be able to meet the needs of all children more effectively.

During the early 1990s some elementary teachers who were interested in more active, manipulative-based mathematics instruction began creating collections of manipulatives and using manipulative-based activities in their classrooms. This led the way to the selection of a mathematics text series that included these strategies within the curriculum.

The NCTM standards and the efforts of other districts to

implement new ways of teaching mathematics prompted more faculty members to explore alternative approaches to the traditional model of math instruction. Teachers enrolled in courses, seminars, and workshops and returned to their classrooms with a wealth of new ideas about how to engage and interest students in mathematics. These strategies made learning more exciting for students and more fun for teachers. Teachers could observe their students making sense of mathematical concepts and processes. Students enjoyed math more because they felt more confident in their own abilities. The strategies themselves were a welcome relief from traditional worksheets for both teachers and students.

Strategies that work pass quickly among faculty members. In Hudson, by the mid-1990s, almost all elementary teachers were using an eclectic mosaic of strategies built on the use of manipulatives. This was a step in the right direction, but did not constitute an inquiry approach to learning.

In the summer of 1995, the district administration encouraged teachers to participate in a locally sponsored Math Solutions course. Almost half the elementary school faculty attended. This course began to shift teachers' conceptual framework from one in which manipulatives were used to represent mathematical procedures to one in which students explored and discussed interesting problems over a period of time. Manipulatives became but one tool to help students conceptualize and represent mathematical ideas. One break-through idea was that these manipulatives have instructional validity not just for primary grades, but for all students. In addition, teachers were able to see the trajectory of conceptual development across the grades, as well as how the foundation of algebraic thinking is built from kindergarten on. The foundation for inquiry-based instruction had been laid.

Ten of these same teachers then attended a summer institute sponsored by the Massachusetts Department of Education as part of the state's National Science Foundation–funded initiative to improve math and science education. For two weeks these teachers were immersed in a new curriculum, *Investigations in Data, Number, and Space* (Dale Seymour, various dates), that brought to bear all they had experienced in their previous courses and workshops but took the final step of providing a consistent curriculum. The district purchased enough materials to pilot-test the curriculum in nine classrooms. However, the introduction of a consistent curriculum built on the new approach created the first tensions among the faculty, some of whom began asking, *Is this a requirement or is it voluntary?*

Choosing a Curriculum

The everyday art of teaching is extremely demanding. In general, teachers do not have the time to reinvent curriculum.

However, they are highly effective in refining implementation strategies and in adapting an exemplary curriculum to their own teaching style and the particular needs of their students. The initial reform had developed naturally as a result of teacher interest and administrative support. Providing a fully articulated curriculum and purchasing the necessary materials was the critical next step. *Investigations in Data, Number, and Space* provided both a model and the tools to begin making inquiry-based instruction a reality in classrooms.

The Math Solutions course had enabled a significant number of teachers to envision what a new mathematics program might look like. For a few this was enough. These teachers fully embraced the inquiry approach to mathematics education and were thrilled to have a fully developed program like *Investigations*. For others, however, it called into question cherished beliefs about mathematics education. These teachers wanted to use the inquiry approach but at the same time hold on to algorithmically based practices. As we encouraged teachers to try more *Investigations* units, these conflicts were drawn into sharper focus.

Providing Ongoing Professional Development

An exemplary curriculum gives teachers the tools they need, but it is only through ongoing professional development that teachers and administrators are able to make effective use of these tools. We've identified four essential elements in our professional development program: opportunities for teachers to engage in mathematical investigations; workshops that stress practical grade-level strategies; an informal support network; and time to learn and reflect.

The majority of teachers in the Hudson school district have now participated in grade-level and cross-grade meetings and workshops sponsored by Northeastern University's Center for the Enhancement of Science and Mathematics Education (CESAME), the regional provider for the state reform initiative; TERC, the authors of the curriculum; and Hudson Public Schools. In these workshops, teachers explore how the major strands of mathematics can be implemented across a number of grades. This understanding is important because introducing a new program means giving up some instructional topics and adding new ones. For example, teachers traditionally have taught two-column addition earlier than it is introduced in *Investigations*. The TERC workshops enabled teachers to see how the *Investigations* conceptual framework is built around a deeper understanding of the structure of the number system and its "landmarks."

Multiple layers of professional development provide entry points for people at different levels of experience with either the approach or the curriculum. We encourage teachers to attend summer institutes both to gain in-depth experience in the approach and materials and to develop general leadership ability. Our teachers attend regional grade-level workshops to share their experiences with teachers in other systems. They also attend regional cross-grade workshops on specific curricular issues. We host on-site consultations with the curriculum developer, as well as district-based, grade-level meetings to work further at particular grade levels. Finally, we provide funding for teachers to work together during the summer in curriculum workshops on such issues as assessment. These are not one-time experiences but rather ongoing programs that continue to refine our work both on the inquiry approach in general and on curriculum implementation.

Change happens in the minds of teachers when they have both the professional development experience and the materials to implement a new approach. Standards- and inquiry-based mathematics reverses the traditional conception of both the purpose for and methodology of instruction. The necessary rethinking entails the personal engagement of teachers in working through mathematical concepts for themselves and then seeing how children come to develop those concepts through curriculum. The interplay between ongoing professional development and trying the curriculum out in the classroom creates opportunities for reflection, problem solving, and personal growth. As a result, adults develop a deeper understanding of mathematics that gives them a clearer window into children's thinking. As one of our teachers has said, "I've learned more about children's mathematical thinking. Instead of relying on one methodology in teaching a specific topic, I've been made aware of a variety of approaches that I feel lead the children and me to deeper mathematical thinking. I now emphasize the necessity of using many strategies to solve problems. Many times the children come up with solutions that I haven't even thought about."

A shift like this takes time. How much depends on a number of variables, including openness to new ideas and prior experience. Each year we survey teachers to assess our progress as well as identify emerging issues. The 1998 *Investigations* survey revealed that some teachers using the program were comfortable with mathematics, while others were not. The *Investigations* curriculum has given the former group new insight into children's mathematical thinking, thereby sharpening their ability to tailor instruction to children's needs. The strongest impact of *Investigations* on the latter group has been with regard to their own comfort and understanding of mathematics. One teacher noted, "I'm beginning to see relationships between numbers I never saw before. I also find myself using landmark numbers to do various operations."

One important way we have been able to move the process of change along is through teacher leaders, who are part of a larger network of mathematics educators in the state. These teacher leaders conduct workshops on *Investigations* in Hudson and around Massachusetts, give support to their colleagues, and take an essential part in planning professional development in the district. These activities, in turn, deepen their own understanding of content, pedagogy, and the requirements for change.

An informal collegial network has also emerged. Teachers with two years or more of experience regularly help out and advise those who are just starting out. They share the lessons they have learned and recount their own struggles in mastering the new approach. These "early adopters," who were willing to try out the new approach without a guarantee of success, are able to build the confidence of the rest of teachers. As one teacher pointed out, "I do feel more confident in my second year. Familiarity with the materials sure helps. The first time through you concentrate on the questioning techniques, the vocabulary, and the format. The second time, the teaching makes sense." The power of sentiments like this, whether garnered in a survey or expressed informally over lunch, at the copy machine, or in the hallway, is twofold. First, they come from trusted colleagues with inherent credibility. Second, they speak to the everyday concerns of teachers.

We are, however, still faced with the challenge of building consistency—involving all teachers in the implementation of the curriculum. For some, it rubs against notions of teacher autonomy and brings resentment. Next year we plan to initiate study groups led by teacher leaders. Each group will identify an area of concern or interest that they want to pursue. We believe this will enable teacher leaders to take a greater role in their own professional growth and that of their colleagues.

Retirements and normal shifts in the teaching population (teachers leave or change grades) require an ever recurring cycle of professional development. Introductory workshops (increasingly led by teacher leaders), on-line grade-level discussion groups, peer coaching, and study groups are some of the options we are pursuing. In addition, we plan to use new professional development programs for teachers and administrators as they become available. Two that we believe are highly effective are *Developing Mathematical Ideas: A Curriculum for Teacher Learning,* and *Administrative Issues in Mathematics Education,* both developed, with NSF support, by the Education Development Center. Multiple venues of professional development are the primary vehicles for carrying us forward.

Building Administrative Support

Reform cannot happen without administrative support. The superintendent's visibility as an advocate for inquiry-based mathematics instruction has been essential in both initiating and sustaining the work of reform. Early on he attended workshops, participated in CESAME meetings, and chaired feedback sessions. Although teachers found this unusual behavior for a superintendent, they felt reassured the administration was going to stand behind the curriculum and those teachers who were trying it out for the first time.

The district principals have also been essential in moving our effort forward. Although they did not attend many of the inservice sessions provided in connection with *Investigations,* they observed the curriculum in action in their classrooms. After doing so, they were convinced of the program's potential and were instrumental in getting it accepted schoolwide. Although they felt the previous program had many strengths and integrated many effective instructional strategies, they observed the shift in both teacher and student thinking that resulted from *Investigations* and placed their support behind the program. Teachers have building-based support for their efforts.

Many teachers have gone through short-lived reform efforts and have developed a degree of skepticism about new programs. The combination of the district's willingness to purchase materials and hire curriculum coordinators to support the teachers' work has added greatly to the credibility of the effort. Existing structures, such as monthly after-school grade-level curriculum coordination meetings, are used for *Investiga-tions*-related professional development and support. Inservice days have also been devoted to the program's implementation. We have been able to convey that this is a districtwide initiative of great importance.

Building Community Support

To ensure that change can survive those in the community who are critical of new programs and methods, the commitment of the local school board is also essential. Throughout our efforts we have had the support of the Hudson School Committee, which tends to be a positive and responsive force for program improvement. This commitment came about both because of the administration's support for the program and because of the interest and commitment shown by the early teacher leaders.

The members of the school committee are kept apprised of the growth and progress of the program and continue to be enthusiastic. Each year, the committee hears presentations from teachers who are using *Investigations*. Even in the pilot year, the superintendent asked a group of teachers to demonstrate the program to the committee. In addition, the committee reviews copies of grant proposals and progress reports before they are submitted. As a result, they have been supportive and encouraging of the move to make *Investigations* the consistent mathematics program throughout the district.

Parents' response to the new approach to mathematics instruction is more complex. Many teachers report that parents are impressed and pleased with their children's new-found enthusiasm for mathematics. On the other hand, they note that parents continue to express concern about mastery of math facts as well as some frustration at not knowing how to help their children with mathematics homework. Unfortunately, we have yet to engage parents in our efforts effectively. Over the next few years we plan to initiate parent math nights and math portfolio presentations that can help parents better understand the program.

Appropriate Testing

The clearest indicator of what we value is what we test. Teachers commonly assess students by a number of informal and formal means. It follows that what we test through high-stakes assessments demonstrates what matters most. Until recently, the primary high-stakes test used in Hudson was the Massachusetts Educational Assessment Program (MEAP). We recognized early on in the *Investigations* implementation that we needed a measure more sensitive to the goals and modes of instruction we were using. At that point we decided to adopt the Terra Nova version of the California Achievement Test as an additional assessment tool. This test is more closely aligned with standards-based curriculum and permits a richer analysis of performance. It focuses more effectively on higher-order thinking and analysis and even provides punch-out manipulatives for mathematical problem solving.

Having data available does not, however, mean that these data will be used for a productive purpose. In general, the education culture is not data or research friendly. Too often assessment data have been used as a political tool of blame rather than as an aid in reflection and improvement. However, in an effort to engage the entire faculty in an analysis of the data from the Terra Nova as well as the MEAP, we turned over grade-level results to grade-level and subject-area faculty committees. Through these committees, teachers have been able to reassess their program and make adjustments to their curriculum. In our recent test results, we have seen improvement in the areas of problem solving, communication, and reasoning. Having a measurement tool that is consistent with an instructional program and that enables teachers to reflect on the quality of their instruction has become an essential ingredient in our efforts to change.

Refining the Design

We have taken a long-term view of change. We know that change is a slow process of ever deepening understanding by faculty members and administrators of the power and effectiveness of a new instructional approach. We walk the sometimes fine line between an imposed and an incremental, faculty-centered approach to reform. An administrative decision by fiat to adopt a new program generates resentment, and the program will be only superficially implemented. On the other hand, both the demands of education reform in the Commonwealth of Massachusetts and our own goals do not permit us the luxury of simply inviting individuals to participate with no administrative imperative.

Our vision and the goals articulated in the NCTM standards require a deep rethinking of the goals and strategies of mathematics instruction. Schools have never before attempted (or felt the need, for that matter) to develop deep mathematical understanding and fluency in all students. Current exemplary mathematics curriculums provide concrete examples within a coherent context. Exemplary curriculums are a necessary but an insufficient step to lasting change. Teachers need to be willing to try out an inquiry-based approach to mathematics even when most colleagues hold to tried-and-true practices. Administrators need to be willing to give support and encouragement to the pioneers along the way.

Moving from an algorithmic approach to an inquiry one involves giving up past practices and trying out new ones. It involves building trust in leaders and early explorers. We recognize that many teachers are not willing to be among the early explorers and that these people base their judgments on long-standing approaches that have been traditionally viewed as successful. Most children have learned math facts and procedures. Just because a few teachers have been willing to try different approaches is not necessarily a persuasive argument for change. These new strategies and goals for mathematics instruction are still viewed through the prism of traditional practices. Our challenge has been to support those who have tried new inquiry-based approaches to mathematics instruction while not leaving the less adventurous behind.

Currently, all of our teachers are trying inquiry- and standards-based approaches to mathematics instruction. Some are convinced of its superiority; others are still skeptical. The progress we have made is a result of the constancy of our vision, the enthusiasm of many teachers, the support of the administration, the resources and leveraging provided by grants, the availability of an exemplary curriculum that models an inquiry mode of instruction, and the opportunity for professional development and dialogue among the faculty.

The next phase of implementation will be equally challenging as we involve all teachers and sustain this involvement over the next two or three years. No curriculum is perfect, and we anticipate that teachers will supplement and revise it to make it work for their students. Our challenge will be to maintain the integrity of the program while enabling teachers to modify and adjust. The key to this next phase will be ongoing faculty support, dialogue, and professional development so that teachers more experienced with the program can help others understand and effectively implement it.

In order to support this process effectively, we have asked our local math and science committee to analyze our annual *Investigations* survey, district assessment data, parent surveys, and teacher feedback and make recommendations for improvements and new implementation strategies.

In Conclusion

Successfully orchestrating systemic reform involves grappling with a few key points. First, we must recognize teachers as learners, who come with preconceptions, interests, and personal goals. An effective professional development program must have direction but also provide a rich array of pathways that respond to teachers' needs. The process is ongoing.

Second, the process is fragile. It involves a complex web

of interdependencies that must be continually attended to lest the entire enterprise falter. However, it is also forgiving. Like bridges built to sway in the wind, it allows for push and pull, as well as mistakes, as long as we are prepared to acknowledge and learn from them. We will need to keep abreast of research on learning, mathematics curriculums, and best practices in professional development. We will need to refrain from developing unalterable commitments to "the way we do things."

Finally, systemic reform means being open to learning about how change comes about. There is no algorithm for reform. At its best it is a collective inquiry into how we can effectively help all children achieve a high degree of numeracy. Keeping that vision and that question in focus gives us the humility and the commitment to sustain our efforts.

Carol A. Balfe
Science Literacy for All Children
5025 Werner Ct.
Oakland, CA 94602